OAXACA
Family, Food, and Fiestas in Teotitlán
CELEBRATION

OAXACA—

Family, Food, and Fiestas in Teotitlán

CELEBRATION

Mary Jane Gagnier de Mendoza

WITH PHOTOGRAPHS BY ARIEL MENDOZA
AND MARY JANE GAGNIER DE MENDOZA

MUSEUM OF NEW MEXICO PRESS · SANTA FE

This book is dedicated to the people of Teotitlán.

Project editor: Mary Wachs
Manuscript editor: Peg Goldstein
Design and production: Deborah Flynn Post
Map: Deborah Reade
Composition: Set in Fairfield with Gill Sans display.

Library of Congress Cataloging-in-Publication Data

Gagnier de Mendoza, Mary Jane.
Oaxaca celebration : family, food and fiestas in Teotitlán / by Mary Jane
Gagnier de Mendoza ; with photographs by Ariel Mendoza and Mary Jane
Gagnier de Mendoza.
p. cm.
ISBN 0-89013-445-6 (paperbound : alk. paper)
1. Festivals--Mexico--Teotitlán del Valle. 2. Fasts and
feasts--Mexico--Teotitlán del Valle. 3. Zapotec
Indians--Mexico--Teotitlán del Valle--Social life and customs. 4.
Zapotec Indians--Mexico--Teotitlán del Valle--Religious life and
customs. 5. Teotitlán del Valle (Mexico)--Social life and customs. 6.
Teotitlán del Valle (Mexico)--Religious life and customs. I. Title.
GT4815.T45G34 2005
394.26972'74--DC22
2005004865

Museum of New Mexico Press
Post Office Box 2087 Santa Fe, New Mexico 87504
www.mnmpress.org

Contents

PREFACE

As a little girl growing up safe and snug in the tiny hamlet of Puce, Ontario, I remember marveling at the exotic, precious objects that lived upon our family's mantel. Surely my father tired of the same questions, but I could never get enough of the images his tales of travel conjured in my mind. After being discharged from the Canadian navy at the end of the Second World War, my father signed on to the merchant marine to escort a destroyer that Canada had sold to China. The journey took him across the Atlantic and through the Suez Canal. Just the names of the faraway places—Rangoon, Singapore, Shanghai—rolled around in my mouth like exquisite chocolate. He would lower a bronze Buddha from the mantel and let me rub its smooth, generous belly. I was allowed to caress the ivory tusks of ebony elephants carved in Ceylon. In retrospect, these innocent moments with my father planted in me the seed of wanderlust that circuitously brought me home.

When Arnulfo Mendoza, the man I eventually married, first took me to meet his family in Teotitlán del Valle and ushered me into a strange room on the western side of the patio, I found myself beholding a wildly adorned altar spanning the entire twenty-foot width of the room. It was early February, and Christmas lights still flashed on and off, synchronized to the squeaky sound of chirping birds. Dozens of scarlet and fuchsia gladiolas flanked either side of the altar, like sentinels guarding the entourage of saints, Christs, and Virgin Marys that hung from the wall encased in tin frames or were housed within wooden niches resting upon the altar. There was fruit on the altar, a lighted votive candle, and a ceramic incense burner.

I had come home. A voice that I had barely understood when I had traveled through India years before now spoke clearly. There was something uncannily familiar about this Zapotec home. Like the Hindus, these people had a direct line with the gods. Faith was not something plugged into for an hour at

Mass on Sundays. Religion was a part of daily life, and it was this comfortable attitude, like the missing piece in a puzzle, that supplied a clear picture of an image I had been struggling to see.

This picture became even more vivid in the months to come. Like the people I had met in India, my new family also took their gods out for walks, changed their outfits, and bedecked them with fragrant jasmine blossoms.

Arnulfo and I—along with our son, Gabriel—traveled to India in 1996. The parallels between India and Mexico constantly intrigued us: the folk culture, the food—curries and moles are first cousins—the crafts, and even the people's physical appearance. But we both agreed that where India consistently scores tens—it is hard to beat bejeweled temple elephants—it also bottoms out with zeros: the poverty, the oppressive multitudes, the filth. Living in this radical flux takes it's toll on the foreigner. Mexico rarely scores above an eight— although exploding fireworks towers rate awfully high—but seldom does one experience anything lower than a two, and this is a livable flux. This is what I have thrived on and what has captivated me for almost two decades.

My mother often says, "Wouldn't it be boring if we knew what life had in store for us." I second that vote, and I accepted, unquestionably, the twist of fate that brought me to live in Oaxaca and marry a Zapotec artist and weaver in Teotitlán del Valle. I remember making a casual pact with fate when we opened our folk art store shortly after our wedding in 1987: I would give Oaxaca ten years of my life. Back then, when I was only twenty-five, ten years seemed like a long time. But those first ten years flew by, and the second decade has been the Discovery Channel turned reality TV. I am asked on occasion to give talks on Oaxacan folk culture and art, and I like to use the image of an

State of Oaxaca

Oaxaca

Teotitlán del Valle

VALLEY OF OAXACA

MEXICO

20 kilometers

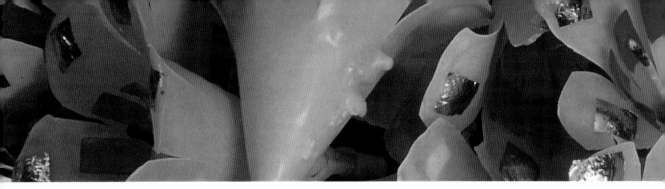

onion to encapsulate this intriguing genre. I try to comfort visitors with the advice that one can experience Oaxaca, its people, and their traditions on an infinite number of levels, like the layers of an onion. Each and every level is perfect in that moment, but do not be deluded—there is always another layer of the onion to peel back, allowing you to go a little deeper, to acquire another perspective.

It is perspective that I offer in the following pages. My perspective, constantly reshaped by my experiences in Teotitlán, has changed radically over the years. I often say, "First I found myself being married in a Zapotec *fandango,* and then I did the research as to what it was all about." This inquiry and search to understand never ends. Even after all these years, every time I get a little smug and think I've gotten to the bottom of it—that I understand what this culture and the traditions mean and where they come from—I invariably see there is a door to open. And when I open it, I see there are ten more doors that need to be opened. This process is good for me. Not only is it humbling, but it also means that the journey is never over!

I invite the reader to meander with me down a path planted with rich fiestas that burst into bloom with dazzling crafts and hang ripe with the fruits of savory cuisine harvested by the sturdy hands of dedicated weavers and steadfast campesinos.

ACKNOWLEDGMENTS

The path to this book has been cleared and lovingly groomed by many people, mostly Teotitecos. In naming names, my list will fall short, but let me try. First and foremost, I thank my husband, Arnulfo Mendoza. If he had not made it so easy to fall in love with him, I'd not have this story to tell. He has been an essential filter for me over the years, helping me understand a world that at times has so perplexed me. *Patience* is a word the people of Teotitlán like to use. With patience, every problem can be solved and every bridge crossed, and this headstrong, impetuous Canadian has tested the limits of Arnulfo's patience. I owe much to my extensive Zapotec family, and the extent of their help will be apparent in the coming pages. I give special thanks to many aunts and uncles: Tía Reyna and Tío Agustín, Tía Emilia and Tío Zacarías, Tía Antonia and Tío Félix. Numerous elders—my mother-in-law, Clara; Tía Natalia; and Marino Vásquez— lent their perspective of time to enrich this story. My sisters-in-law showed me from the very beginning proper Teotitlán etiquette and culinary traditions. While cousin Reyna cooked up inspiring sustenance, she was always close by to verify and correct. Domingo Gutiérrez shared his knowledge of Teotitlán history and his grandmother's memories of village life. Innumerable dancers, clowns, musicians, and candle makers lit up countless fiestas over the years.

Good friend and fine photographer Ariel Mendoza has been staunchly dedicated to this project since its inception in 1999; he arrived before dawn and stayed until the band played the last dance. His photographs capture the exuberance of Teotitlán in all its festive glory. My dear friend Shelora Sheldan shares my passion for Oaxacan cuisine and gave a workable form to the traditional recipes. Do try them! Doe Coover lent wise advice. Kate Regan, Carol Waterbury, and Lynn Foster read the manuscript from all perspectives and lent their sage insights.

My gratitude to my mother, Jean Gagnier, and to my editor, Mary Wachs, for believing in the importance of bringing this book to life.

DECEMBER 16–24: PRE-CHRISTMAS POSADAS

Nightly candlelit processions, accompanied by brass bands, parade the statues of the Virgin Mary and Saint Joseph through the streets.

CHRISTMAS EVE

In an elaborate procession, participants carry adorned beeswax candles, and the statue of baby Jesus accompanies Mary and Joseph. The procession ends at the church with midnight Mass.

CHRISTMAS DAY

In the morning, the *padrinos* (godparents) of the baby Jesus return to church to receive the statue, and then return to their home. A band accompanies the procession, and children gather to break piñatas at the *padrinos'* home.

NEW YEAR'S EVE AND NEW YEAR'S DAY

Villagers make a pilgrimage to Guibla Xnuax to make petitions to the Virgin for the new year.

JANUARY 13–14: FIESTA OF THE BLACK CHRIST/ *FIESTA DEL CRISTO NEGRO DE ESQUIPULAS*

The market is busy, with intense trading of *flor de cacao* blossoms and black-bean tamales. On the night of January 13 and the following day, Teotitecos visit the homes of family and friends who have statues of the Cristo Negro de Esquipulas. Fiesta food is prepared, and brass bands frequently play in homes.

FEBRUARY 2: LA CANDELARIA

Village women go to the church to have their lavishly dressed statues of the infant Jesus (now seated in a chair) blessed by the priest. The priest also blesses seeds, most often ones saved from the previous harvest to be used in the upcoming planting.

LENT AND HOLY WEEK (Variable dates)

Every Friday between Ash Wednesday and Palm Sunday features a morning procession through the village. Parents accompany numerous children dressed as angels. A brass band plays.

PALM SUNDAY

Following morning Mass, a procession takes the statue of Jesus as San Salvador riding a burro from its niche in the church. Beyond the walled courtyard, it makes a reentry symbolic of Jesus entering Jerusalem.

HOLY MONDAY

From morning until evening, a procession of penitents and faithful accompanies the emotive images of Christ carrying the cross and the grieving mother as the Virgin of Solitude. At twelve stops, neighborhood residents offer refreshments and snacks to the participants.

HOLY THURSDAY

The afternoon features a reenactment of the Last Supper in the rectory of the church. In the evening, the community visits a statue of Christ carrying the cross, placed in an improvised jail cell in the northwestern corner of the churchyard.

GOOD FRIDAY

In the morning, a procession known as *el encuentro* ("the encounter") departs the church in two separate groups, one with the statue of Christ carrying the cross and the other with the Virgin Mary, Mary Magdalene, and Saint John. Both processions meet up in the municipal plaza near noon. A solemn evening procession accompanies a statue of the crucified Christ to the cemetery.

DANZA DE LOS VIEJOS
(Monday–Friday following Easter Sunday)

Each day, one of the town's five *secciones,* beginning with *primera sección,* hosts the Danza de los Viejos (a carnival-like fiesta featuring masked elders). The public portion of the fiesta is celebrated in the early evening in the municipal plaza, with a brass band, masked dancers, and snack stalls.

MAY 3: FIESTA OF THE HOLY CROSS/ *FIESTA DE LA SANTA CRUZ*

The fiesta features an organized race to the top of Xiabets. The faithful also make a pilgrimage to the top of the sacred mountain.

JUNE 24: FIESTA OF SAINT JOHN/ *FIESTA DE SAN JUAN*

This day features horse races in the streets between the church and the morning food market.

FIESTA OF THE PRECIOUS BLOOD OF CHRIST/ *FIESTA DE LA PRECIOSA SANGRE*

(Variable dates; the principal feast day falls on the first Wednesday in July, provided the prior Sunday also falls in July)

On Monday and Friday at approximately 5:00 p.m., a *convite* departs the church. More than one hundred colorfully dressed señoritas carry baskets supporting religious standards on their heads. The troupe of *danzantes,* two brass bands, and the Church Committee accompany this parade along the principal procession route of the village. On Tuesday and Saturday at approximately 11:00 p.m., villagers attend a fireworks show in the churchyard. Pyrotechnic puffballs called *bombas* explode in the night sky, and village men concealed inside of papier-mâché dolls, turkeys, and bulls dance to the music of a brass band while fireworks explode from these figures. *Danzantes* perform *Danza de la Pluma* Wednesday and Sunday.

SEPTEMBER 6–8: FIESTA OF THE VIRGIN OF THE NATIVITY/ *FIESTA DE LA VIRGEN DE LA NATIVIDAD*

September 6 features a *convite,* September 7 features fireworks and the *Danza de la Pluma* in the afternoon, and September 8 features the *Danza de la Pluma* in the morning and afternoon.

FIESTA OF THE VIRGIN OF THE ROSARY/ *FIESTA DE LA VIRGEN DEL ROSARIO*

(Variable dates; the principal fiesta falls on the first Sunday in October, provided the prior Friday also falls in October)

A *convite* is held on Friday, with fireworks on Saturday night and the Danza de la Pluma on Saturday afternoon and Sunday morning and afternoon.

NOVEMBER 1: ALL SAINTS' DAY/ *TODOS SANTOS*

On the late afternoon of October 31 the spirits of deseased children return to their homes where miniature altars have been made to receive them.

NOVEMBER 2: ALL SOULS' DAY/ *DÍA DE MUERTOS*

At 3 p.m. on November 1 the souls of adults arrive. Special food is prepared and Teotitecos spend the next 24 hours attending to both the visiting spirits and the living who come to pay their respects. This is an intimate family fiesta until 3 p.m. on the 2nd when many villagers go to the cemetery to see off the spirits with live music and libations.

LOS RESPONSOS (Variable dates)

One Monday in November is designated for *los responsos* (prayers for the dead) in the village cemetery.

DECEMBER 11–12 (Every third year) FIESTA OF THE VIRGIN OF GUADALUPE

On the eve of the feast on December 11, the community marks the end of the troupe of *danzantes'* term with an extravagant celebration in the open courtyard of the church. Hundreds of relatives of the *danzantes* participate in the event. A brass band plays; dances are called, and women dance with lacquered gourds stacked with sugar flowers and candies, which they share with the other participants and observers.

DECEMBER 12: DANZA DE LA PLUMA

In the courtyard of the church, on the morning and afternoon of December 12, the *Danza de la Pluma* is performed for the last time by the departing dance troupe.

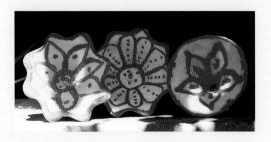

A masked buffoon prances through the streets during the devotional parade for the patron saints.
Gagnier de Mendoza.

INTRODUCTION

For almost twenty years I have lived *Mexican fiestas* through
the pulse-beat of Teotitlán del Valle, a village fifteen miles east of the city
of Oaxaca. I wed my husband, Arnulfo, and buried my father-in-law,
Emiliano, here. Each May 3, Arnulfo and I host the Fiesta of the Holy
Cross, a role my mother-in-law, Clara, a seasoned veteran in the Zapotec art of
hosting, introduced me to.

On countless occasions I have stirred enormous caldrons steaming with
enough glistening *mole negro* to feed five hundred. I can't count the times we
have risen before dawn to attend a fiesta, or how many times at a fiesta I have
dutifully taken another Teotiteco's hand in mine, bowed my head, and uttered
the ceremonial greeting *chxan*, the word for God. There is a blur of blessings:
blessing the betrothed, blessing the gifts, blessing turkeys adorned with cigarettes and fuchsia bougainvillea necklaces; called upon to bless the mole, bless
the bread, and bless the chocolate.

My husband is the eldest son, and since his father's death in 1991, he has
become the ceremonial head of the family. As his wife, my position carries a
similar stature. At fiestas, my mother-in-law routinely calls me into the kitchen
to sit with the important señoras. I get the relatively effortless job of stacking
large plates with towering mounds of freshly baked *pan dulce* (sweet bread),
along with steaming cups of hot chocolate—a lush brew of liquid dark chocolate laced with ground cinnamon. I have become good at this task, although
I still must check my innate desire for efficiency and slow my pace to that unhurried tempo, aptly coined "Zapotec time" by a friend. Nothing exemplifies this
vast pooling of collective efforts more than a fiesta, and ample hands translate
into a rhythmic, unhurried pace.

Shortly after I married in 1987, I found myself seated among a group of women, helping prepare the meal at a fiesta. I remarked that it would be faster to simply chop the oregano, instead of picking the tiny leaves one by one from the stock. While the aunts and cousins acknowledged the truth of my suggestion, they were swift to point out that here speed was not the objective. There were plenty of hands eager to remain busy, and weren't they enjoying each other's company, savoring their easygoing time together?

I arrived in Teotitlán inept at making tortillas, an intuitive ability acquired only through arduous repetition commencing at an early age. While I appreciate a certain Zen-like state attained in this repetitive labor, I admit that my interest leans more to theory than practice. And it was rapidly apparent that my business skills and command of English were far more valuable traits to put to use—especially considering that I had six strong and able unmarried sisters-in-law to provide the staples of the daily meal.

At a social gathering not long after our wedding, some village men prodded my father-in-law regarding the culinary abilities of his new daughter-in-law. When asked if I could make the decidedly difficult oversized tortillas called

Dozens of ceramic bowls await serving. *Gagnier de Mendoza.*

tlayudas, my proud and noble father-in-law was quick to defend me—as much saving his own face as mine—by proclaiming that while I did *not* make tlayudas, I *was* accomplished in the enigmatic art of baking birthday cakes. A hush went over the table, because most village ovens are used only for storing utensils and linens. Making birthday cakes is left to a handful of professional bakers.

I first won acceptance into the community at a festival in the mid-1980s. I was invited to play my clarinet with the brass band that accompanied the Danza de la Pluma, a sizable honor considering that bands back then included only men. The people of Teotitlán have been gentle in judging me, and it was apparent from the outset that they applied different rules to me than to themselves.

When I came to the village, women didn't drive, something I had done since my teens. But shortly afterward, my sister-in-law Marcelina became one of the village's first women with a license. I happily report that these days, long braids interwoven with thick satin ribbons are a common sight behind the steering wheel. Women here do not ride horses, but I regularly ride ours through Teotitlán's breathtaking countryside, where I might encounter Tío Agustín tending his

One band heads up the *convite* while another comes in tow. They often play entirely distinct melodies simultaneously. *Gagnier de Mendoza.*

Teotitlán, meaning "place near the gods" in Náhuatl, the language of the Aztecs, is nestled on the edge of a valley dotted with ancient ceremonial sites. *Ariel Mendoza.*

fields or our neighbor Erasto shepherding his cattle and sheep on the rocky foothills that rise to the north. A cheerful wave from these weathered hands makes for a comforting encounter, and while I am careful to blend into social events, wearing appropriately conservative dress including a full bib apron, these sensitive people understand the cultural leap implied by a Canadian girl marrying into a Zapotec Indian village, and they know that total assimilation is unrealistic.

The older women often remark that they couldn't imagine going to live someplace as far away as Canada, and even after seventeen years of marriage, an aging aunt might still ask at a fiesta if I have become accustomed to life in Teotitlán. The answer is that I have walked a delicate tightrope, with one foot anchored to my own roots and the other immersed in Teotitlán, cautious not to fall in headfirst. This distance, perhaps a necessary survival tactic, has allowed me to retain my identity, run a gallery in the city of Oaxaca, and stay connected with my family and old friends. This distance has also allowed me a unique perspective from which to observe, yet participate in, the dynamics that charge festival life.

回回回

I first came to Teotitlán in 1985. It was an early February morning, the mist still sleeping on the valley floor, as the blaze of sunrise crested the Sierra Juárez straight ahead. It must have been serendipity that music brought me to this town. I was traveling through Mexico with my clarinet, and radical changes in humidity had sent it into a consternating nosedive of squeaks and squawks. The night before, I had encountered a man seated across from me at El Sol y La Luna, a popular club in Oaxaca. I really couldn't ignore him; he had a long black ponytail, wore a black fedora and a black leather jacket, and ordered a black coffee with *piquete,* a sting in the form of a shot of *mezcal.* He told me he was a painter and weaver, and I told him I was studying music. And so the ailing clarinet came up in the conversation, and this intriguing man offered to introduce me to a couple of clarinetist uncles in his village the next morning. "I'll come by your hotel at 6:00 a.m." were his parting words. How generous on his part, but I figured the *piquetes* were talking, and I said my skeptical good-byes.

Rustled from her sleep in the tenuous light of dawn, the overtly annoyed señora who ran the hotel gave a loud rap on my door, announcing that a man in a green Gremlin was asking for me. That is how I found myself traveling down the southeastern arm of the Oaxaca Valley with Arnulfo Mendoza, turning north to his ancient village of Teotitlán del Valle.

This town is home to a community of Zapotec weavers, inhabitants of the region for more than three thousand years. In the fifteenth century, Aztec invaders named the village Teotitlán, meaning "place near the gods," a reference to the potent idols housed on the immense stone peak that keeps watch over the village. Myths surround this powerful site, known in Zapotec as Xiabets and best translated as "Brother Mountain." Some call Xiabets the second home of Quetzalcoatl, the pre-Hispanic plumed serpent god. Another legend says that thousands of years ago, when the Zapotecs were still nomads, they received a prophecy that they were to stop wandering and settle in a place where a great blue bird appeared on a mountain peak illuminated by the light of the full moon. The blue heron winters in the nearby wetlands, and the people of Teotitlán believe the mountain in the legend is Xiabets.

Weaving is an ancient craft in Teotitlán, and pre-Hispanic documents detail how villagers sent lengths of woven cloth to Moctezuma's empire in Tenochtitlán as tribute. Sometime in the Spanish colonial era, the upright pedal loom was introduced to Teotitlán, and sarape weaving joined subsistence farming, creating a way of life little changed over the centuries. But in the past thirty years, the individuality and quality of Teotitlán weavings have won them an international following among collectors, and market demand has significantly raised the village's standard of living. The handwoven rugs of Teotitlán are featured in fashionable stores from New York to Santa Fe. Weavers in India and Bulgaria reproduce these traditional Zapotec designs. In 2003 *Smithsonian* magazine devoted twelve pages to Teotitlán weaving in an in-depth article called "Dream Weavers." Teotitlán weaving spans the gamut of cost and quality, from economical saddle blankets sold on the Texas border to silk and wool tapestries exhibited in museums and prized by serious collectors. With a population of more than eight thousand, and practically every person over age fifteen participating in the weaving process, Teotitlán may very well be the largest hand-weaving community in the world. Mass migration to northern Mexican border towns and beyond has left innumerable communities in the state of Oaxaca virtual ghost towns, marginally populated by only the elderly and women with children. Yet Teotitlán enjoys a thriving permanent population. Pickup trucks traverse the newly cobbled main street, Avenida Juárez, lined with costly brick buildings touting smartly painted signs announcing "100% wool handwoven Zapotec rugs."

Teotitecos are by nature hardworking. Although Agustín Ruiz, my uncle by marriage and a man in his mid-sixties, is a successful rug seller, he can be

A silk and wool weaving, inspired by nineteenth-century sarapes, from Arnulfo
Mendoza's atelier. *Claudio Sanchez.*

found most mornings tending his cornfield and edible nopal cactus patch. After a hearty mid-morning breakfast, he spends the rest of the day dyeing yarns, weaving, or packing orders for shipment. Weaving has unquestionably overshadowed farming from an economic viewpoint, yet the majority of Teotitecos still plant corn, beans, and squash once a year. Most plow their fields with oxen and harvest corn by hand, with oversized reed baskets strapped to their backs. Agustín sees the profits from rug weaving as a boon from God, a blessing that could disappear at any time. Farming, on the other hand, is a way of receiving and honoring the gifts of Mother Earth. "Working the land keeps us humble," affirms Agustín.

This eternal tradition, rooted here since time immemorial, blends seamlessly with contemporary life, creating a lifestyle that has held my admiration for almost twenty years. Spend a day or two in Teotitlán, and you are likely to see one of the village's five full brass bands lead a procession, festive or funerary, toward the village's colonial Catholic church, whose main nave is lined with exquisitely adorned beeswax candles. Just steps away, the regal women of Teotitlán gather each morning in the market, finely woven baskets loaded with squash

Teotitlán's colonial church, with recently excavated pre-Hispanic ruins in the foreground and the sacred peak Xiabets in the distance. *Ariel Mendoza.*

blossoms, nopal cactus pads, and savory grasshoppers—traditional foods for millennia—tucked under their arms. It is this undercurrent of the ancient, a backbone of purpose and place, that sustains the Teotitecos' fiestas.

Their harmonious coexistence with tradition and change has left me with a lasting impression since my very first visit. Here, economic prosperity does not supplant tradition but further enhances it. This new affluence has embellished the fiestas, long the mainstay of the village's spiritual and social life, and with good economic times the fiestas have become even more exuberant and theatrical. Today the celebrations not only mark Teotitlán's renaissance but also serve to bridge past and present, ancient and modern, pre-Hispanic and Christian.

And what makes this phenomenon even more impressive is that Teotitlán is not a remote, isolated hamlet but is only fifteen miles from the city of Oaxaca, the state capital and a popular tourist destination with a population of more than four hundred thousand. Of all the towns within the same radius of the capital, Teotitlán is among the few that has perserved its native Zapotec language, largely extinct among neighboring villages. Although the Zapotec that villagers speak is not a written language, its tenacious presence in village ceremonies, internal politicking, and home life shows how the people of Teotitlán, steadfast in preserving traditions, navigate the incursions of modern Mexico.

꠱꠱꠱

The word *fiesta* is synonymous with Mexico and embodies an essence, a spirit that leaves a "party" simply pale by comparison. This is not to say that Mexican fiestas are always grand in scale, but they are grand by intention, by the energy exerted, by group cooperation and collective goodwill.

Throughout Mexico, fiestas create and sustain a sense of belonging within the extended family, the church, and the community. Individuality dissolves to unite in the collective identity, whether people are joining forces to prepare a wedding feast for hundreds or parading in a *convite* (a devotional procession for a local patron saint). In Teotitlán, where kith and kin vie with one another for sales of rugs and the attentions of wholesale buyers, fiestas create a defined neutral time and space, exempt from business competition. Here, commerce is set aside, and villagers pool efforts for the collective good of the community.

Indeed, the people of Teotitlán refer to participation in a fiesta as a *compromiso*, best explained as a social and moral duty, an obligation to accompany and attend but also to take part in the work. To pierce the complex reality of fiesta life in Teotitlán, it is absolutely essential to lay aside the somewhat erroneous

The altar at the author's home in Teotitlán. *Ariel Mendoza.*

concept of Mexican fiestas as nothing more than merriment and frivolity. A tremendous collective effort is employed; order, ceremony, and ritual rule the day, whether villagers are celebrating a son's marriage or a saint's feast day.

My husband never took me to a Teotitlán wedding until I found myself being married to him in one. Maybe he had an inkling that I would have insisted on a tidy elopement had I known what awaited me. We were wed at 8:00 a.m., and the last dance ended at 3:00 the following morning. The day before, the flourish of activity had included the blessing and slaughtering of pigs. The day after, the band returned and there was dancing again.

We all have pivotal moments, indelible events that changed us forever. Just after dawn on our wedding day, I remember kneeling with Arnulfo before the Mendoza family altar. There we received individual blessings from his family members, followed by my family and our friends, who mimicked the Zapotec ritual that culminated with the gentle knocking together of our heads. During those long minutes, the thought took hold that now I was married, that the ensuing church ceremony was superfluous, perfunctory, and that what really counted had just happened.

The Teotitlán story is an inspiring example that has changed my way of living. There is no one-size-fits-all lifestyle, and my challenge has been to adapt

The author and her husband, Arnulfo Mendoza—just married in 1987.

the lessons offered by the Teotitecos—whether about preparing food with joy and goodwill or about bringing modified Zapotec celebrations to my reserved Canadian family—to my own reality.

We celebrated my mother's seventieth birthday in Oaxaca. She flew down, as did a handful of family members. We hired a live marimba band, hung strings of festive *papel picado* (cut-paper flags) in the patio, mixed up fresh mango margaritas, and to fill up the place, invited more friends and family from Oaxaca. My mother blew out her birthday candles and laughed so much that her cheek muscles ached the next day. In getting up to dance, she forgot the weight of her years, and tears were just behind my smile when she confided that this was the first real birthday party she had ever had. She was not talking about an intimate family gathering with a nice dinner and birthday cake; she was talking about a fiesta, and she felt very special having those who love her make so much effort on her behalf. This is a lesson I learned from Teotitlán.

卐卐卐

For the Zapotecs of Teotitlán, nothing is too good for their gods, and in great measure similar exigencies apply to how they celebrate themselves. Whether in the home, the street, or the church, one is constantly reminded of the plenitude of elaborate artistic expressions. Inside their colonial church, stunning floral arrangements frame statues of old, venerated saints; in every home, fresh flowers adorn family altars. For hours on end, the *danzantes*, Teotitlán's famed dancers with magnificent plumed headdresses, entertain the heavenly powers, performing strenuous leaps and turns beneath the imposing facade of the colonial church. Village bands are in constant demand: leading up street processions, churning out hours of traditional music at family fiestas, or accompanying religious ceremonies.

Teotitlán's traditional cooking, especially the cooking of fiesta foods, is a sophisticated art form. Just skimming the list of foods uncovers such notables as rich *mole negro* composed of no fewer than fifteen different ingredients; incredibly delicate *tamales de mole amarillo*, creatively wrapped in corn leaf ribbons—perhaps the closest we get to pre-conquest food—and mysterious, little-understood *chocolate atole*, served up in bright lacquered gourds with hand-carved stirring sticks.

The fragile, adorned beeswax candle—a singular example of village artistry and a fascinating expression of ritual craft—spans fiestas, religious and secular, public and familial. As a maximum statement of ephemeral beauty, the intricately decorated, meter-tall tapers appear by the dozens to embellish the side altars of the church, illuminate the procession of the baby Jesus on Christmas Eve, or overflow from private altars at the complex ritual of marriage negotiations.

Little known to outsiders, Teotitlán preserves the ancient tradition of masking. On a handful of occasions throughout the year, village-carved wooden masks transform their wearers into wise ancestral spirits or comical buffoons.

Fireworks are a favorite part of fiestas, and there is no example of this ephemeral art form more breathtaking than the *castillo*, a four-story pyrotechnic tower synonymous in Mexico with patron saints' celebrations. Teotitlán will spend upward of five thousand U.S. dollars on each of the four *castillos* set alight every year for the patron saints' fiestas.

░░░

Fiestas offer important opportunities to socialize outside the family, especially for women. While informal visits do occur, they usually involve some underlying motive, such as asking a favor or seeking advice. Within the village,

The masked *viejos* greet Arnulfo Mendoza during the Fiesta of the Holy Cross. *Ariel Mendoza.*

It takes two to stir the pot. Señoras improvise with bamboo poles to churn a caldron of bubbling mole. *Ariel Mendoza.*

socializing is largely reserved for fiestas, times when diverse cross sections of the population unite: working, eating, and drinking together, often for days at a time. These are opportunities to catch up on local news, exchange ideas, and, especially for men, debate village politics.

Firmly established moral codes inherent in rural Oaxacan communities clearly demarcate socially acceptable behavior—especially for women. Whereas it is normal for young men, even those who are married, to hang out with *primos* and *amigos* on street corners, a proper señorita would be severely criticized for doing the same. The public space outside the security of the walled family compound is seen as "uncertain"—fertile soil for gossip and speculation. Just as the home equates to safety, trust can be truly achieved only in the close relationship of family and kin. Even sophisticated, well-traveled Teotitecos such as my husband admit that close friendships don't come easily; he is most comfortable with the camaraderie of relatives. But solitude is not a concern in a village like Teotitlán, where families are large and migration is limited. By middle age, the average Teotiteco has dozens of cousins, equal numbers of nieces and nephews, and probably five to ten *compadrazgos*—relationships with the godparents of one's children or the parents of one's godchildren. This network translates into a vast social circle of well over a hundred people.

In spite of Teotitlán's phenomenal economic success, one shouldn't assume that moneymaking dictates its actions. Villagers have an elaborate unwritten order of priorities, and looms will stand still while weavers fulfill social obligations at a fiesta that could easily demand several days of participation. Reciprocal participation is the energy that fuels extravagant fiestas. In this community, where extended family translates into considerable human resources, it is unheard of to hire waiters or have an event catered.

Days prior to a fiesta, young men make forays into the nearby mountains for firewood, filling pickup trucks with logs to fuel the endless cooking. The men's other primary chore is bringing in extra reserves of water, pumped from plentiful wells into barrels in the back of pickups, then siphoned off to cisterns for use at the fiesta.

For major fiestas such as weddings, more than a thousand handmade tlayudas will be consumed over several days Participants eat some at the fiesta, but they take many away, along with other generous leftovers, to share with their families and neighbors. Nearby vacant lots or flat rooftops, shaded by rigged-up tarps, become workplaces for dozens of young women churning out these immense tortillas. They work in two-person teams, one grinding the masa and pressing it into twelve-inch circles, while her partner cooks the tlayudas, turning and flipping them to leathery perfection. Fit women in their prime kneel in rows to work the *metates*, stone-grinding everything from chiles to chocolate, an activity that maintains toned arms and a strong spine. Older, married women take charge of other aspects of the cooking, such as stirring the huge caldrons bubbling with yellow, black, or red *moles*, adding rich chicken or turkey broth for the perfect consistency. Hierarchy sends the most honored guests to the kitchen. Here, important woman, godmothers and grandmothers, aunts and sisters, sit on comfortable little chairs or more traditionally nestle on mats on the floor, overseeing the allocation of sweet breads and hot chocolate. Certain women become associated with specific tasks—Tía Emilia is renowned for beating chocolate to a thick froth. There is a job for every woman, from the pre-pubescent girls who mind the younger children, hoisting them on nonexistent hips, rehearsing for their futures, to the most ancient *abuela,* who melts into a warm corner of the kitchen, called upon to dispense her sage blessings on the bread, chocolate, and mezcal.

Cooking, an extraordinarily time-consuming process at Teotitlán fiestas, keeps women in constant activity. It seems that dishes from the morning meal are no sooner washed than the cycle begins afresh for the afternoon repast. Since men rarely venture into this domain, they find themselves with ample hours for animated discussions, enlivened by rounds of energizing mezcal and thirst-quenching *chelitas*—six-ounce bottles of Corona beer. Traditionally, women serve males of the household in everyday life, but the exception rules at fiestas, where young men attend to older male guests. These same young men also serve the women, who by necessity eat last.

An interesting idiosyncrasy of native fiestas in the valley of Oaxaca involves the dishes. It is perfectly normal, even expected, for every married woman to have ceramic cups, bowls, and plates for fifty—if not one hundred—guests, items often acquired as wedding gifts. Disposable plates are rarely encountered; they are too flimsy to hold the weight of turkey legs and dense moles. Cutlery has little use in this culture, and table etiquette is measured by how adeptly one maneuvers the deftly folded pieces of tlayuda used to scoop up sauces. To avoid potentially disastrous splashes of mole, people hoist meat out of the sauce to an awaiting tlayuda and use other pieces of tlayuda to pull apart the meat. In fact, the tlayuda raises the concept of "disposable plates" to resounding ecological heights, since this sturdy, versatile tortilla acts as both edible plate and spoon.

By no means do I pretend to paint a Zapotec utopia. Teotitlán fiestas are no perfect garden parties; they are in fact long, tiring social marathons. Rather, I hope to present one community's way of celebrating life, through which people acknowledge life's fragility and understand the importance of living more fully in the present.

An analogy as simple as a corn plant encapsulates the entire premise of this book. If you visit Oaxaca in October, you are sure to observe dried stalks of corn still standing in the fields. Yet on these "dead" sentinels, dried kernels cling to the cobs, holding within their nuclei the divine energy to repeat an endless cycle. The course of human life is mirrored in agriculture. Seeds are planted in the humid earth, soon banked to the tender stalk; black beans later climb the sturdy plant; finally, the rains cease, and both are left to dry against the highland sun, where once again the seeds await their reunion with the earth.

By refusing to allow life's important moments to slip away ignored—whether the birth of a child or giving thanks to the gods, burying their loved ones or welcoming their return as spirits—this community lives very much in the present, supporting each other in joy and sorrow. My intention in the following pages is to guide the reader on a journey through time, along a year interwoven with festivals. Some are fixed celebrations honoring the gods. Other fiestas mark a member's ascent through the community. I do not set out to catalog every celebration in Teotitlán; that would take tomes. Rather we will meander down this passageway of events, opening doors and stepping in on fiestas that have quickened my heart, nourished my soul, and brought tears to my eyes. This is what I have to offer. I hope to illuminate an ancient yet vibrant model of living that can inspire others to reap the rewards rooted in the conscious effort to sustain community and celebrate life.

Midnight Mass. *Ariel Mendoza.*

Chapter 1

COMMENCING THE CYCLE:
CHRISTMAS POSADAS AND THE NEW YEAR

Mexican Catholics live intimately with their gods. They dress them up, parade them about, and offer them food. On countless occasions, I have encountered wooden statues of Christ and the Virgin with their toes actually worn away by centuries of devout kisses. I harbor a secret envy for these sincere expressions of love, grateful all the same to find myself yet again enveloped in the candlelight warmth and goose bumps of another Teotitlán fiesta.

In much of Latin America, nine days and nights of fiestas lead up to Christmas Eve. These events, known as posadas, reenact Mary and Joseph's journey to Bethlehem, culminating on the eve of December 24 with the birth of the baby Jesus. With love and devotion, the people of Teotitlán open their doors to the Virgen María and San José, offering them "lodging," which explains the term *posada*.

Emilia González and her husband, Zacarías Ruiz, clearly remember the details of the posada they hosted in 1990. Hardworking weavers and successful rug wholesalers, they were living comfortably and had recently finished building a large new home. As is common for couples who have gained a certain economic stability, it was time to give thanks to the gods for their fortunate situation. Emilia said that by hosting the posada, by actually having the Virgen María and San José spend the night on their shiny tiled altar, under their newly constructed roof, they would receive the ultimate blessing and protection for both family and home.

Four months before, the handsome couple had signed up for one of the nine posadas. In Teotitlán, even so-called minor fiestas like posadas are extravagant by most outside standards; the planning and logistics require considerable amounts of both time and money. So starting in the early 1980s, Emilia and Zacarías began giving *guelaguetzas.* Not to be confused with a folkloric dance festival in the city of Oaxaca, guelaguetza is best explained as a private, internal loan system whereby items of fixed value are given and received.

For example, if you give two hundred tlayudas in guelaguetza for a neighbor's fiesta, you will get two hundred tlayudas back from that neighbor for your own fiesta. Each family maintains its "savings and loans" ledger, writing down accounts of all guelaguetzas in detail—from the weight of a turkey to the quantity of tlayudas; the date of the guelaguetza, and who it was given by or received from. Many couples begin giving guelaguetzas years before they may need them, often saving for a son's wedding when the child is still in primary school.

A decade or more may go by before families "call in" their guelaguetzas. Should the recipients of guelaguetzas die before repaying their "loans," the outstanding guelaguetzas are passed on to their principal heirs, usually the eldest son. Similarly, heirs inherit the benefits of their parents' accredited guelaguetzas. Only a few years ago, my mother-in-law notified Arnulfo and me that we needed to purchase a twenty-pound turkey to repay a guelaguetza that had been made for our wedding in 1987.

※※※

Emilia and Zacarías had chosen the fifth posada, and as December 19 approached, they called in their guelaguetzas: turkeys, sugar and cacao, corn and tlayudas. The couple had calculated carefully, budgeting for every detail, and after subtracting all the guelaguetzas they had given out over the years, they could pretty much estimate the hard cash still required. By this system, the heaviest expenses for the fiesta were covered, and with their savings they bought the remaining ingredients. The food served at the posada would include one hundred turkeys bathed in velvety mole negro, four hundred eggs scrambled in chicken broth for *higadito,* and the rare and costly beverage chocolate atole.

Both Emilia and Zacarías come from large families, and a month earlier they had made customary visits to immediate family, inviting parents and siblings, aunts and uncles, compadres and godparents. We were among the nieces and nephews invited. The word *invitado* translates as "guest," but in Teotitlán it also means someone who partakes in the workload. Some invitados, mostly women, started arriving days before to help Emilia with the laborious preparation of the mole

Tia Emilia beats chocolate.
Gagnier de Mendoza.

Sweet bread and chocolate.
Gagnier de Mendoza.

Toasting chiles on the *comal.*
Gagnier de Mendoza.

negro. Pounds of chiles, almonds, sesame seeds, and raisins were set in constant motion on the hot *comal* (clay griddle) and carefully toasted to perfection. Garlic and onions were buried in hot ashes and roasted by glowing embers. Nowadays, ingredients are ground at the neighborhood *molino* (mill), but had this mole been prepared back in the 1950s, a team of strong young women, kneeling at stone metates, would have spent hours doing the same task by hand.

At seven o'clock on the evening of December 19, Arnulfo and I joined dozens of other invitados, mostly married couples. All the women carried candles elaborately adorned with flowers and birds. Sheltering with the palms of our hands the fragile flames that lit our measured steps, we followed the music of a full brass band to the house where the Virgen María and San José, affectionately called "the pilgrims," had received posada the night before. These were not just wooden statues of Mary and Joseph but seemingly living beings, very much part of the lives of the people of Teotitlán. The procession had come to escort these special guests to their next posada.

With a mixture of honor and responsibility, Zacarías and Emilia received the three-foot-tall pilgrims into their charge. When the band broke into an

A street procession with San José and the Virgen María during the pre-Christmas *posadas. Marcela Taboada.*

upbeat Sousa march, both santos, richly costumed in velvet and brocade, were raised in their individual palanquins, and the journey continued to Emilia and Zacarías's home. Once the statues were safely delivered to the family altar, bejeweled for the occasion in tiny flashing lights, the band knelt before the statues and for the better part of an hour sang to them. Later, as the invitados filed past to greet the Virgen María and San José, kissing their feet or hands in reverence, the musicians exchanged their singing for familiar band melodies.

Manuel Ruiz, Porfirio Carreño, and Macario Bazan then entered the altar room. Their hands were clasped passively, the body language of respect. They approached the two wooden statues and bent to kiss their bases. They exchanged solemn greetings with the hosts. This trio, the *alabanceros*, the singers of prayers called *alabanzas*, wasted no time in commencing their job; they dropped to their knees, and a polyphony of deep, slow melodies emerged, expanded, and enveloped the room.

With soul-piercing harmonies, their sounds transcended time and space. They appeared to have a direct transmission to the heavenly powers, a supersonic connection with God, sometimes imploring but most often singing prayers of devotion. As the alabanceros continued their harmonies, the ubiquitous mezcal, hot chocolate, and sweet bread energized the gathering through the late night hours. Some guests began trickling home around midnight, but it was 5:00 a.m. before the alabanceros finished chanting; quiet fell upon the home, and scant rest came to the weary hosts.

The invitados began returning with the dawn, and after greeting first the pilgrims and then the hosts, men took their places at long tables lining the altar room. Women put on aprons, a sure sign there was work to be done No ordinary breakfast could be served with the Virgen María and San José as houseguests; this meal was to honor the parents of the soon-to-be-born baby Jesus. Bowls of regal chocolate atole, set on platters toppling with fresh sweet breads, were served to all the invitados, followed by *higadito*, the ultimate Teotitlán breakfast dish of eggs and chicken scrambled in a rich garlicky cumin broth.

▨▨▨

The members of the Church Committee are the real movers and shakers of the religious fanfare associated with the saints in the church. Teotitlán still subscribes to an early colonial system of internal self-governing called *usos y costumbres*, literally "uses and customs," whereby men are assigned to numerous village committees, donating their time and labor for the collective benefit of the community. The committees are numerous—Potable Water, Garbage Collection, and

Community Health being but a few. A committee term can last up to three years, but the *cargo* (obligatory service) is so demanding for the Church Committee that every year the town names new members. Former members are allowed to "rest" for an equal period before being assigned another *cargo*.

The Church Committee is comprised of thirteen members, a number symbolic of the twelve apostles plus Jesus Christ. They take their cargo very seriously, especially the president, treasurer, and secretary, who are required to make major organizational decisions, manage vast quantities of money, and draw up public announcements. Each committee member is responsible for maintaining one and sometimes two altars within the church, which involves buying huge bouquets of fresh flowers for the altars on a weekly basis as well as heading up processions on saints' respective feast days.

Throughout the year, the Church Committee acts as guardian of the statue of the baby Jesus. But on December 24, the *padrinos del niño Dios* (godparents to the baby Jesus) take possession of the statue. In 2000, after years of anticipation, Benjamín Ruiz and his wife, Gloria de los Ángeles, are finally the padrinos. This sponsorship is one of the most coveted *mayordomías* in Teotitlán—spoken for up to six years in advance—not some fiesta for a minor saint but a direct show of adoration for the infant God.

On this morning, the padrinos head up the procession, escorted by a brass band, the shrill strains of the *chirimía*, and a rambunctious throng of village children. They arrive at the church, where the Church Committee is waiting. Gloria, standing beneath the protection of a brocaded satin canopy, receives the statue of the baby Jesus on a tray covered with a new Yves Saint Laurent print scarf.

The procession returns to the padrinos' home at a snail's pace. As it nears the bustling morning food market, both men and women line up, eager to show their adoration and receive the blessings of the infant God. Gloria carries the baby Jesus with overt solemnity; she and the rest of the entourage stop as the faithful approach to kiss the statue and leave some coins of offering on the tray.

Vivid piñatas, hung in the middle of the street just outside the padrinos' home, offer a joyous reception to the procession, returned from a successful mission. Mobs of children take turns swinging wildly at the suspended piñatas. Finally, after several tries, a youngster smashes one open; sticks of sugarcane, peanuts, and candies scatter to the ground, and chaos breaks out in a free-for-all scuttle to grab the most. When the last of a dozen piñatas are scattered over the street in shards, the padrinos treat the delighted children to rice pudding and sweet tamales laced with cinnamon and raisins. Gift giving is not part of the native Mexican Christmas. Instead, Mexicans find joy in the shared experience and the collective celebration.

On Christmas Eve day, the godmother carries the baby Jesus in her arms.
Ariel Mendoza.

December 24 is a day of fasting and vigil. The villagers eat no meat, and compared to the extravagant food prepared for the previous nine posadas, the menu is simple. People eat black beans and white corn atole for breakfast. A dish called *pescado envuelto* (batter-fried salted fish in a broth with white beans) is typically served on Christmas Eve.

The baby Jesus spends a relatively quiet day by himself, nestled on the padrinos' altar. But by evening, his parents, María and José, have arrived, seeking their final posada—the symbolic manger where the baby will be born. By 8:00 p.m. the gathering has swelled to include the band, the hosts, the invitados, and of course the pair of wooden pilgrims, ready to accompany their baby to midnight Mass. This time the procession makes no beeline to the church. Instead it weaves its way for hours, through all of the town's five neighborhoods. Standing in their doorways, entire families wait anxiously for the passing of the Diosito, an endearing term for "little God," and the fortuitous opportunity to kiss the statue. A mother carries her toddler to the baby Jesus, and the little one instinctually drops her lips to the miniature wooden foot.

Hours later, by now nearing midnight, the procession finally enters the churchyard. The Virgen María and San José appear to levitate on the covered palanquins, bobbing in an ocean of indigo blue rebozos (shawls). Gloria takes her role seriously, holding the baby Jesus tightly in her arms. At the church's entrance, Padre Rómulo greets the procession. He welcomes equally those of flesh and those of wood, who together file up the main aisle, lined with the godparents' kneeling invitados. Like sentries on guard, the invitados hold before their faces not rifles but fantastic candles adorned with wax angels, flowers, and birds. Flanked by the golden glow of a hundred candles, this retinue proceeds

Teotitecos feel blessed to kiss the baby Jesus. *Ariel Mendoza.*

with the formality of ancient courtiers. The padrinos safely install the sacred family on the church's main altarpiece, now transformed into a two-story Nativity scene landscaped with fresh moss, exotic bromeliads, and babbling brooks.

At the end of Mass, village children dance as the band plays, and the solemnity gives way to a festive air. I pick out my nieces Silvia and Clara, dressed in the traditional costumes of *pastorcitas* (little shepherdesses). Small boys dressed as shepherds hold staffs and water gourds, and several *angelitos* (diminutive angels), clad with authentic chicken-feather wings, add to the evening's theatrics.

Octogenarian Antonia García is a wealth of village history and has passed down much evanescent information to her grandson Domingo Gutiérrez, an activist in preserving Teotitlán culture. She has told him how, in the early part of the twentieth century, the *mayordomos* (sponsors) of the Virgin of the Nativity hosted a fiesta on the evening of Christmas Day—ancient reverence for Mother Mary. Domingo glows as he passes down her vivid descriptions of how the esplanade of the church would ignite with the arrival of dozens of ribbon-braided señoras, a dazzling sight with their candy-flower-filled *jicapextles* (lavishly lacquered calabashes) perched upon their shoulders. The band would play, and dignified Teotitecos, respected men and women, would dance late into the night to celebrate the birth of their infant God.

▱▱▱

Dusk has fallen on New Year's Day, and since time immemorial, the people of Teotitlán have gathered on a barren hillside just beyond town to bear witness to the renewal of each new year.

It is here, in this place, that Mother Earth meets the mother of God, and they become one again. On New Year's Day in 1987, a village youth, Manuel Mendoza Lazo, accidentally dug up a crude stone figure. My uncle Agustín Ruiz is certain the effigy is ancient; villagers even call it sacred, and since its discovery, the little "mother goddess" has resided on the altar in a small adobe chapel erected here. Seated next to Tío Agustín, Arnulfo elaborates: "We call this site Guibla Xnuax, Zapotec for 'the rock near the woman Mary.' Our elders tell stories, passed down to them by their elders, that once, before we counted time, an image of a woman appeared, bringing with her great waters from the stream. But our people did not give her due respect. They ignored her, so one day she left. She simply disappeared. Only then did we begin to worship her, making pilgrimage to her place every New Year, in hopes that she would return." According to another local legend, hundreds of years ago a statue of the Virgin Mary miraculously appeared in the same riverbed. Many believe she is the more ancient woman returned. "This is why we make our petitions to the Virgen María on New Year's Day," says Arnulfo.

This place is referred to in Spanish as the *cuevita* (little cave), but really it's not a cave at all, just two modest hollows in the stone wall of a ravine. Both indentations house crosses and have become New Year pilgrimage destinations. Arnulfo explains, "We mark sacred places with a cross. We could not leave a precious statue unprotected in the open—someone might steal it—but a couple of sticks of wood are safe. The form of the cross was prevalent in pre-Hispanic culture. Just look at the patterns carved in the ruins at Mitla. We believe it represents the form of man and our link with God."

It is here that entire families line up, patiently awaiting their turn at the shrine, kneeling, pausing for a moment, dropping a few coins onto the collection tray. What do they pray for? The words of Emilia González speak of both change and continuity, a cultural symbiosis adeptly maneuvered by most Teotitecos: "It is perfectly fine to ask for money, and the way we did this a long time ago was to scrape the shalelike rock at the shrine into a red calabash to catch the shavings. How full you filled the bowl represented how much money you were asking for." In age-old tradition, Emilia and her family, like the rest of Teotitlán, still line up to show their respect by bowing down to kiss the crosses. But nowadays they invoke their petitions for economic prosperity by lodging several paper bills of tiny play money in the spaces between the crosses and the wall.

Open hills rise up on either side of Guibla Xnuax, and by late afternoon on New Year's Day a multitude of curious mounds dots the fallow earth. But closer observation reveals tiny constructions, miniature houses built from fieldstones, rocks, and pebbles. The community makes these objects as requests to the Virgin for the coming year.

Anyone visiting Teotitlán can testify that building is a village passion. It seems as though villagers never really finish constructing—there is always the need for a larger weaving workshop, a new rug showroom, or an addition for a recently married son. Yet Emilia clarifies, "We do not always build homes at Guibla Xnuax. They are just what you see the most." She explains that they also make miniature farm animals: "If a woman wants more chickens, she shapes them out of the *bejuco* plant, or if she needs more eggs, small flower buds are used. Childless couples ask the Virgin for a baby, modeling the tiny form from earth."

▭▭▭

New Year at Guibla Xnuax. *Ariel Mendoza.*

Music is a constant at Teotitlán fiestas. The origin of Teotitlán's musical proliferation goes back to the 1920s, when musician Edmundo González formed and conducted the first band. According to family history, Simón Ruiz, my husband's great uncle, first brought a band out to play on New Year's Eve in 1935, and he and his invitados danced for their gods under the night sky's infinitely starlit firmament. Simón loved music, yet his idea took decades to become a tradition, and only since the 1970s has the Committee of Guibla Xnuax hired one of the village brass bands to enhance the festive ambience each New Year.

Teotitlán boasts five twenty-plus-piece brass bands, with music for every occasion. Under the shade of the church's ancient laurel trees, for hours at a time, a band might accompany the danzantes' rigorous leaps and twirls with the rhythms of waltzes, Spanish *jotas*, or *pasos dobles*. Bands' stirring dirges accompany funeral processions—the deceased's final walk through town. On Good Friday, the tension-charged cacophony of two bands, simultaneously playing distinctive melodies, announces the emotional last encounter of the statues of Christ and his mother, Mary. The versatile bands can accompany street processions for hours, walking in the heat and dust. At weddings, band members sit from dusk to dawn, playing *jarabes*, dances that can last up to thirty minutes. Every New Year's Day, a band plays on a small, flat esplanade, flanked by rough-hewn log benches, and the men of the committee invite family, friends, visitors, and the faithful to celebrate through the night with music, dancing, and libations.

In contrast to the brass band's lively dances, the penetrating harmonies of the alabanceros float through the doorway of the tiny adobe chapel. Although adobe gives the building a weathered air, Arnulfo explains that it was built only recently, to give the alabanceros someplace to direct their chanting: "They couldn't simply stand on the hill and sing to the sky. See how they kneel and chant before the little altar?"

With the comfortable informality of a country outing, probably well over a thousand have flocked to this rocky hillside, and many will stay well into the first night of the new year. As the golden moon rises out of the eastern mountains, bonfires illuminate family gatherings. Youths hurl balls of fire—made from ultralight *zompantle* wood soaked in kerosene—high into the night sky, like shooting stars. As I sit enveloped within this scene, with the sounds of congenial Zapotec conversation blowing in the breeze, I allow myself to momentarily relinquish time, submersed in this ancient rite. When I do float back, I don't need to see them—I know they are there—a confounding array of cars and trucks parked just over the crest, a symbol, I remind myself, that this tradition is alive and in the making.

The *alabanceros* direct their chants of devotion to the image of the cross, a generic form representing the sacred. *Gagnier de Mendoza.*

Petra González carries poinsettias for her altar. *Gagnier de Mendoza.*

FIESTA OF THE BLACK CHRIST OF ESQUIPULAS

t is January 14 and almost noon when I enter the well-illuminated municipal market. The first thing that hits me is something just shy of a mob scene. A crowd of village women, usually so orderly and polite, is pushing and shoving to get close to a young man holding a small basket high above his head. Like spontaneous combustion, this same scene ignites, to greater and lesser degrees, throughout the ample midway. I am with Reyna Mendoza Ruiz, my cousin by marriage. Almost amused by the spectacle, she explains that the baskets he and other vendors hold contain the culprit of this commotion—a tiny white aromatic blossom known as the *flor de cacao.*

To set the story straight, the *flor de cacao* isn't the true blossom of the cacao tree, a plant that grows nowhere in the Oaxaca Valley. It got its name because it smells like chocolate and is an essential ingredient in *tejate,* a hardy native beverage made of ground corn and cacao beans.

On most days, the market is virtually deserted after a couple hours of fervent morning activity. But today is the eve of the Fiesta of the Cristo Negro de Esquipulas (Black Christ of Esquipulas), and that changes everything. The women of Huayapan, a village about nine miles down the valley toward Oaxaca, are famous for their *tejate,* and most of these villagers enthusiastically cultivate the *flor de cacao* in their gardens.

For much longer than anyone can remember, each January 14, villagers from Huayapan have come to Teotitlán to trade the fragrant white blooms, which Teotitecos thread into garlands for their statues of the Black Christ of Esquipulas, whose feast they celebrate the following day. Days after the fiesta has ended, women remove the garlands from their statues and save the dried blossoms, which in the coming months they will add to *tejate* like a spice.

On this day, the intense demand has shot prices as high as five pesos for six flowers, and the Municipal Market Committee has had to enforce cost controls. This mercantile phenomenon occurs but once a year, and to my knowledge only in Teotitlán.

The buzz of activity continues outside the market, where women stand behind wheelbarrows stacked with thick-skinned, oversized grapefruits, ripe oranges, and sweet mandarins. The exotic *zapote negro* is conspicuously prevalent today; this soft, rotund fruit is sweetest when the glistening black flesh almost oozes from its bright green skin. Most of the fruits and flowers for sale in the market today have come from the gardens of Teotitlán.

In exchange for their flowers, the women of Huayapan return home with their baskets laden with unique black-bean-filled tamales, prepared only in Teotitlán. In Teotitlán itself, virtually every family feasts on this simple yet delicious specialty on this day. While the ingredients are common enough—corn masa and a black-bean paste—it is the painstaking preparation that puts this *tamal* in a class of its own.

Outside the morning market, village women sell rosemary, tuberoses, and poinsettias to adorn altars for the Black Christ of Esquipulas. *Gagnier de Mendoza.*

Women making *tejate* for a fiesta. *Gagnier de Mendoza.*

Flor de cacao blossoms. *Gagnier de Mendoza.*

How deftly Reyna, her mother, and her sisters work. Their long, strong strokes grind the corn masa to a velvety smooth consistency. They press it into delicate disks and spoon a seasoned black-bean paste down the center, finishing the process by carefully folding in both sides of the crepe-thin dough. Reyna gently lays this incredibly fragile creation, only a fraction of an inch thick, into a corn husk cradle lined with a licorice-flavored native avocado leaf. Dozens upon dozens of these boat-shaped tamales are steamed to mouthwatering perfection and served with an earthy salsa of fresh garlic and smoky *pasilla* chiles, grown only in the remote Mixe region of Oaxaca.

Like keeping time by a clock, you can identify a fiesta by the way the villagers decorate their altars. Following tradition, on this day we fill the vases on our altar with bouquets of *nochebuenas* (long-stemmed poinsettias native to Mexico), coffee branches hanging heavy with ripe red fruit, and stems of fresh-cut rosemary used exclusively as an ornamental or healing herb. How contented our Black Christ looks residing in his vintage niche dated 1969, escorted by a panoply of perfumed tropical fruits and flowers.

Almost one thousand miles away, hidden in a lush tropical valley on the far eastern border of Guatemala, the town of Esquipulas is home to the original statue of the Cristo Negro. Latin America flourishes with pilgrimage sites, guardians of miraculous icons such as the passionately venerated Virgen de Juquila in southern Oaxaca. The journey to Esquipulas is no light undertaking, and the pilgrimage is most often the result of a *promesa*, a pact made with the divine powers.

A promesa could be called a bargaining tool used with the gods. As an example, parents might implore the Black Christ to heal their gravely ill child. In return for this "favor," they "promise"—thereby the promesa—to make a pilgrimage to Esquipulas in gratitude for the Lord answering their prayers.

Agustín Ruiz tells the story of his father's pilgrimage to Esquipulas in 1923: "My father, Antonio, was just fifteen when he left with another señor from the nearby town of Tlacolula. They met up with other pilgrims along the way, and the group grew bigger. When money ran out, he stopped, and he worked building the road that would become the Pan-American Highway. The faith of pilgrims is great, and my father was sure no one would turn him away when he knocked on strange doors, looking for shelter for the night. He walked the entire distance. It took him six months to reach Esquipulas and six months to return."

A niche for the Cristo Negro de Esquipulas from the author's family altar. *Gagnier de Mendoza.*

Chintextle: The Pilgrim's Chile Paste

This is a pungent chile paste. A little goes a long way. It's excellent spread on hot tortillas with sliced avocado, strips of grilled beef, or chicken. Roll up and enjoy.

3 *pasilla* chiles, seeded and deveined
3 medium *guajillo* chiles, seeded and deveined
4 garlic cloves with skins on
7 medium-sized tomatillos (approximately 7 ounces), husks removed and rinsed
salt to taste

> Heat a cast-iron griddle or pan over medium heat; toast chiles evenly, taking care not to burn them.
> Soak chiles in hot water for approximately 20 minutes, or until soft but not mushy.
> While chiles are soaking, toast whole garlic cloves on the griddle, turning occasionally until soft.
> Allow garlic to cool; peel off skins.
> On the griddle, roast tomatillos until light green, soft, and charred in spots.
> Drain chiles. Blend with garlic and tomatillos to a smooth, thick paste. Add water as necessary to release blades of blender.
> Salt to taste.

The salsa will thicken with refrigeration. Thin it with a bit of water before using. It will keep refrigerated for one week.

Grinding *chintextle* on a stone metate. *Gagnier de Mendoza.*

Agustín made his own pilgrimage to Esquipulas almost fifty years later. When he departed, the alabanceros accompanied him with chanted prayers until he reached the edge of town.

In 1997 Clara Ruiz, Agustín's sister and my mother-in-law, decided it was time for her to visit the Cristo Negro de Esquipulas, to carry out a promesa she made with her husband, Emiliano, many years before he died. She would travel with her six unmarried children. A month before Clara embarked on her pilgrimage, she ordered a specially made beeswax candle—simple, unadorned, and weighing more than four pounds. Careful not to leave anyone out, she visited the homes of family and compadres. Standing before their altars, with God and all the saints as witness, her relatives first kissed the candle, then Clara rubbed the taper over each person's body, giving special attention to areas of sickness and pain. She took it to Esquipulas, and by lighting the candle before the venerated Cristo Negro, it became a spiritual go-between, having absorbed the faithful's wishes and in turn conveying their needs to the icon. If you see it as they do, it is not so much that God answers the prayers but that the statue, infused with the powers of the god it represents, actually works the miracles.

Milagro means "miracle," and in Mexico *milagros* are images, usually made from metal, in a multitude of forms including men and women, arms and legs, horses and pigs, beans and corn, babies and burros—the list goes on and on. Just about anything or anyone who needs the intervention of the divine powers is good subject matter for a *milagro*. Customarily, Teotitecos wear their respective *milagros*—of a man, woman, child, or baby, suspended from a cotton string—for up to a month before a relative's departure for Esquipulas. They believe that during this time the *milagro* takes on the essence of the wearer, who then entrusts it to the departing pilgrim, with instructions to hang it within the holy sanctuary, thereby creating an effect similar to that of the candle.

Clara was given small amounts of money to leave at the holy shrine, or to help with the journey's expenses. As her departure day neared, neighbors and relatives arrived with stacks of fresh tlayudas. My sisters-in-law had gathered provisions, fixing the standard pilgrim's fare of hardboiled eggs, quick-cooking toasted cracked corn and beans, cured meat, and *chintextle* (a pungent paste of *pasilla* chiles, garlic, and sometimes dried shrimp). The women of Teotitlán are particularly fussy about eating food from other villages—never as well prepared or properly seasoned as their own native dishes—and to avoid disappointments along the way, the pilgrims packed their vehicle with sacks of village-grown corn for making tortillas, a charcoal-burning camp stove, and essential utensils for outdoor cooking.

As they had innumerable times in the past, the alabanceros arrived before dawn. Their plaintive harmonies combined with the evocative scent of burning copal lent to the farewell a ritual ambience inseparable from the traditions of Teotitlán.

More than a month later, Clara and her children returned from their pilgrimage to Esquipulas. In strict observance of traditional protocol, the devout entourage did not go directly home. Clara's daughter Rosario had called ahead from the Isthmus of Tehuantepec to notify her married brother Jacobo of their approaching arrival. That single telephone call initiated a well-rehearsed flourish of activity that within forty-eight hours converted a one-time rodeo ring on the outskirts of town into an open-air reception hall of sizable girth. The site was bedecked with a yellow-and-blue-striped circus tent and dozens of rented folding chairs.

The alabanceros were back again; the band had assembled, and extended family numbering a hundred strong turned their expectant gazes to the south-

A niche with the Black Christ de Esquipulas. *Gagnier de Mendoza.*

eastern horizon, searching for a sign. On the edge of a new millennium, in the midst of a desolate cactus-covered expanse, through a fine dust haze, a Ford Windstar emerged along the ancient road, the southern entrance to the village since pre-Hispanic times.

The pilgrims had returned with absolute proof of their religious journey, and an impromptu outdoor altar was erected for their recently acquired Cristo Negro. The carved wooden statue—much more than a religious souvenir—had been blessed in Esquipulas's massive basilica, imbuing its essence with a measure of the divine. Through a curtain of purifying incense, the alabanceros kept up a vigil of sacred chants throughout the night, while extended family lined up with fresh flowers and votive candles to pay their respects to the dearly venerated religious icon. The characteristic ritual sustenance of hot chocolate and sweet bread, never to be lacking, fortified the participants through the chilling winter night, while free-flowing mezcal fueled the internal fires.

Mass was organized for the pilgrims the following morning, and the village priest officially received Clara and her children, bestowing them and their new statue with added blessings. Only now, with the church formalities complete, could the travelers finally return home, where a full-blown fiesta was in the works. I never stop marveling at this community's immense wealth of human resources, at its matter-of-fact approach to preparing caldrons of delicious, steaming food to feed hundreds. Such was the case this day, and with ample reason for celebration, the band played throughout the day and into the night. Overjoyed to be home and surrounded by family, the seven pilgrims shared the spotlight, dancing the traditional two-step *jarabe,* each donning a straw hat fancifully decorated with tiny lacquered gourds and colorful ribbons, a ubiquitous and absolutely essential purchase for every visitor to Esquipulas.

Brimming with emotion, the pilgrims burst with colorful travel stories, tales of the Cristo's miracles and the wonders of Esquipulas's healing clay. Even in these economically flush times, the people of this community seldom "take vacations," perceived as idle, flippant behavior. Although decades have passed since the last Teotiteco walked to Esquipulas, women, more so than men, still see the unknown beyond home and village as potentially perilous territory. Yet there is no disguising the excitement when you hear Teotitecos speak of their journeys to pilgrimage sites, and it strikes me that this community has discovered a cultural loophole that combines stimulating travel with spiritual pursuits.

Looking like stalactites, dozens of tapers await adorning by Viviana Villalobos. *Ariel Mendoza.*

Chapter 3

PREWEDDING RITUALS

On May 4, just as dawn was breaking, Josefina and Eduardo knocked on our door. I remember the day clearly because they had been with us the night before, celebrating our yearly Fiesta of the Holy Cross. There was an aura of agitation in their movements—I don't think they had slept much—and as is the custom, we ushered them directly into the altar room. We addressed each other as *compadre* and *comadre,* since Arnulfo and I are the godparents of their youngest children, fraternal twins Eduardo and Rocio.

But today the conversation turned directly to their middle daughter, Cristina. The night before she had been "stolen"—the literal translation from the Spanish *robar.* It really means that she had secretly slipped away to her awaiting boyfriend, and he in turn had taken her back to his home, where he still lived with his parents.

In truth, none of the above is very strange. In fact, this same chain of events occurs all the time in Teotitlán, where young couples, having successfully hidden their courtship, routinely do away with long engagements in the village's own version of elopement. At a prearranged time, when everyone is asleep—or in this case when her parents were at our fiesta—the girl sneaks away from her house to join her awaiting boyfriend. After consummating their passions, the boy takes her to his home, awakens his parents, and presents them with his wife-to-be.

Being "stolen" has become over the last fifty years standard custom, and very likely the girl's own mother did the same thing. Nevertheless, the ensuing ritual, Chisiak Lazá, translated literally from Zapotec as "to content," can be best understood as a means of appeasing or contenting the girl's parents, and it refers to their distraught state upon discovering their daughter's disappearance.

Once the event takes place, sparks fly as the wheels of communication are set in motion. The boy's parents immediately call their *huehuete* to notify the girl's parents of their daughter's whereabouts. Like an intervillage messenger service, the huehuetes herald intimate news between families, mediating engagements and wedding arrangements. They are the go-betweens and the consummate masters of ceremony. Like ambassadors, they attend to the ceremonial and ritual requirements of the village on a secular level, acting distinctly outside the official Catholic Church. At wedding celebrations, with the exception of the church ceremony, they take charge of all formalities.

When the huehuete visited Eduardo and Josefina, hours before they came to see us, he spoke to them in the highest form of ceremonial Zapotec. He assured them that their daughter was safe and would be well cared for in her new home. The following morning we accompanied Josefina and Eduardo, along with a dozen or so of their close relatives, for the huehuete's scheduled return, but this time accompanied by their future son-in-law's parents. The express purpose of this visit was to set the date when they would officially return "to content."

When I talked with a former priest of Teotitlán about this matter, he condoned the custom of a couple living together before being formally married in the Catholic Church. He said he much preferred this custom, because when the couple did choose to be married, they knew they were well suited for each other, and divorce was unlikely to occur. Matrimony, he reminded me, is one of the seven Holy Sacraments, while living out of wedlock is merely a corporal sin. Although a church wedding may not take place for several years after the elopement, this doesn't mean that Teotitecos frequently change partners. It does happen on occasion, and there are single mothers in the village, but by no means is this the status quo.

Some couples prefer to adhere to the older traditions, and in recent years more and more young people have opted for a formal engagement, with the boy openly asking for the girl's hand in marriage rather than carrying out the secretive and impromptu alternative.

◻◻◻

Antonio Ruiz and Claudina Lazo had decided on a traditional engagement. Testing unsure waters, before Antonio broached the topic of a wedding with his own parents, he had already proposed marriage to Claudina, and she had accepted.

Receiving blessings, 2005. *Gagnier de Mendoza.*

Decorated beeswax candles are the principal gifts for marriage negotiations. *Ariel Mendoza.*

During several informal visits, the two families worked out details and chose a date several months off for the ceremony to content. Emilia, Antonio's mother, counted eighty-seven married couples on her guest list. Each couple would be responsible for one candle.

Teotitlán's unique candles figure into many ceremonies but the ritual to content is by far the most touching. The candles' exquisite beauty helps heal the parents' wound at the loss of their daughter when she leaves home. My gentle, soft-spoken uncle by marriage, Januario González, remembered his own feelings when his daughter eloped twenty years before: "When they presented us with the candles, their light and the beautiful sweet-smelling pure beeswax represented our daughter Marina, and for many months we kept a candle lit in front of the altar as a symbol of her." Whether the loss of a daughter is the jolting experience of having her "stolen" or the anticipated loss of her leaving home after a formal engagement, the girl's parents must be contented with this ritual.

As Teotitlán has grown economically stronger, fiestas have become ever more opulent, and candles have played a major role. Emilia González remembers that thirty-five years ago, her fiancé's family gave her parents only fifteen two-pound candles as part of the prenuptial negotiations. How fast things change. Just one generation later, she volunteers with pride and disbelief, they presented some eighty candles to content the parents of her son's future bride.

Tucked away on a rough dirt side street, hidden behind a nondescript facade, Viviana Villalobos, sorceress of beeswax, sits immersed in a contemplative state of creation. You could say that Viviana was born with beeswax in her blood. She comes from three generations of Teotitlán candle makers. Under the tutelage of her grandmother, Viviana began honing her craft as a girl of eight years.

During one visit with Viviana, she was preoccupied with her immediate task—creating a massive candle weighing in at seventeen pounds, specially ordered for a ceremony to content So large was the taper that only by climbing onto a chair was Viviana tall enough to pour wax over its six-foot height. From a well-worn gourd, she poured the molten liquid in one long, smooth, continuous rhythm, steadily building up the candle's girth.

The next time I came by, Viviana was making wax lilies. To build up the ideal thickness, she alternated dipping a cone-shaped cedar mold from hot wax into cool water three times. It intrigued me how she popped the mold into her mouth and gave it a quick roll around before bathing it in molten wax. All trades have their tricks, and she explained that the saliva provides a necessary film to loosen the wax from the mold, which had been carved by her grandfather thirty years before.

Viviana Villalobos uses a chair to reach the tips of her largest candles. *Ariel Mendoza.*

Practice makes perfect, and only by repetition can the craft of candle-making be learned. *Ariel Mendoza.*

The dozen-plus village candle makers produce all their own molds and understandably covet them. From the clay molds emerge miniature pineapples and mangos, guavas and apples, ducks and birds—decorative elements to be affixed to large tapers. The smooth round bottom of an old clay cooking pot acts as a mold for giant pink dahlias. Bright red roses and fragrant day lilies spring to life from curved and conical carved wooden molds.

A candle's most important single element—and the most detailed—is the angel. It is always placed at the candle's base, with little arms rising overhead to visually sustain the rest of the wax decorations. Viviana reminded me that this image echoes the way señoritas carry adorned baskets upon their heads during convites. Viviana also showed me that the wax angel decoration is a girl, unmistakably feminine, with her hair neatly parted down the middle. When candles are given to content, the angel symbolizes, and attempts to replace, the daughter who no longer lives at home.

The diminutive angel sustains the lavish decorations. *Ariel Mendoza.*

Some molds go back generations, a source of pride and originality. *Ariel Mendoza.*

Invitados divide the gifts among themselves. *Ariel Mendoza.*

The day had come to content, and typical of Teotitlán organization, all the relatives, including Arnulfo and me, had gathered just before dawn at Emilia and Zacarías's home. On this third Sunday in February, in the morning's first tenuous light, I found my place among the married women, whose candles were light enough to carry in hand. As we started off on foot, I checked my steps to find that familiar but inherently unnatural pace of unhurried activity. Once I settled in, bound for Claudina's parents' home, I found myself enjoying the moment as we floated through the deserted streets, proudly bearing our magnificent waxen standards.

The morning sun was just rising as we arrived at our destination, and a caravan of pickup trucks laden with the remaining gifts followed in tow. As the baskets, cases, crates, and bundles were ferried from the trucks to the altar room, the parents of the bride-to-be, Braulio and Soledad, in the company of dozens of their extended family members, observed the spectacle from the patio of their home. Solemnity reigned as the minutes ticked by. The ensuing pageantry and fanfare resembled the grandeur of dignitary visits from times long past.

Fruit is a timeless symbol of offering in Teotitlán. Even in everyday life, a gift of fruit is instinctively placed upon the family altar. Fruit is a principal component of prenuptial negotiations, and the quantity and quality given are seen as a gauge as to how much the prospective bride is appreciated and valued. On this Sunday morning, it was very clear that Claudina was worth a great deal.

The list of fruit read: fifteen hundred oranges, twenty-eight cases of imported apples, two hundred plantains, two hundred pineapples, and two cases of melons. Sweet bread made up the remaining bulk of the offering, and Emilia's kitchen could have been a wholesale bakery that morning, containing by her estimate more than two thousand *pan dulces*. They had purchased one thousand, and the rest had come from their extended family, which was expected to contribute fruit or bread, as well as ceremonial candles.

Fifteen enormous baskets of bread, large enough to comfortably conceal an adult, were staggered and stacked down the center of the room, in a two-story island faced by the altar. The baskets held traditional sweet breads such as *pan de cazuela* (bread knots filled with chocolate swirls), the rich egg and butter bread called *pan de yema y mantequilla*, and *marquesotes* (spongelike loaves created to soak up hot chocolate).

Only a portion of the fruit could fit in the room after all the bread and candles had been arranged. Balanced atop several cases of apples were two of the largest jicapextles I had ever seen, and Emilia confided to me she had personally toasted the forty-four pounds of cacao beans used to make the chocolate contained within. As a climax to the display, the best had been saved until last. Twelve live turkeys, feet bound together, were laid down like tribute before pre-Hispanic royalty. As an encore, Antonio, the fiancé, entered toting a bundle of firewood and a broom, symbolic of the chores he would perform for his future in-laws in the five months leading up to the wedding.

You might be wondering what on earth Braulio and Soledad would do with all the bread and fruit. This rite is not lost to Teotitlán's intrinsic tradition of reciprocation. Later that day, after the future groom's entourage had departed, everyone got to work dividing up the bounty among themselves. Each of the dozens of married couples returned home with their own sizable basket laden with perishable gifts, which they in turn shared with neighbors and relatives. In exchange, each couple would be responsible for a gift on Claudina's wedding day.

Everyone was in awe of the event. This was quite possibly the most lavish ceremony to content ever witnessed in the community. "How the times have changed," I heard people say. "We were all poor before," agreed the older señoras seated around a large table, little room-temperature Corona beers in front of each. They shook their heads, and as though still trying to make sense of this day's opulence, they reminisced, "Only thirty years ago, twenty candles, five baskets of bread, and even one case of apples were fine offerings." And again, as on

Specks of gold leaf embellish wax lilies, one of the candle's most traditional ornaments. *Ariel Mendoza.*

Chocolate and sweet breads. *Ariel Mendoza.*

Each married woman in Teotitlán owns many hand-embroidered *serviettes* and sturdy woven baskets, loaned and always returned for ceremonial occasions. *Gagnier de Mendoza.*

countless occasions, I was impressed by how Teotitlán navigates change. Instead of letting tradition capsize in the waves of modern Mexico, Teotitecos harness prosperity to further embellish their customs.

Once the eighty-seven candles were all arranged before the altar, and the bread and fruit had been stacked down the middle, there was not much free space left in the room. But somehow we all filed in, Antonio's family packed in on one side of the great wall of bread and Claudina's family lined up on the other. The traditional greeting of *chxan* was exchanged with a respectful bowing of the head. During the ceremony, staunch tradition prevailed as both families' hue-huetes commanded the order of events, much as they have been done for generations. The field of wax candles threw a luminous glow over Claudina and Antonio as they stood before the altar to receive the huehuetes' solemn words. Except for the frequent interjection of "Jesucristo" and "Santísma Virgen María," both men spoke entirely in Zapotec. They invoked for the future couple the blessings of the gods and alternated warnings with sound advice. At the command of the huehuete, Claudina and Antonio sank to their knees. Each and every relative from both families, first men and then women, filed by to give blessings and counsel. Some women went on at length about the duties of being a daughter-in-law, about making a new life, about obeying a husband and in-laws. A great deal was said about duty and respect toward each other, parents, and in-laws and about patience and understanding. In Teotitlán, as in much of indigenous Mexico, the newly formed couple begins life together not only in the groom's parents' home but also under their direct authority. It often takes years for the couple to be granted their independence and move to a separate home.

The village elders delighted in recounting how things used to be. Claudina's elfish grandmother, Refugia González Sosa, age seventy-three, grew up in a family of pork butchers. Refugia's was an arranged marriage, and the lengthy engagement was to ensure that the couple had adequate time to learn to get along. Her betrothal lasted three years. During that time, her future husband came to her parents' home daily to carry buckets of water, chop firewood, and learn butcher's skills. As tradition dictated, he swept the patio and the street in front of the home every Wednesday and Sunday.

More than fifty years later, on May 15, 2001, Antonio Ruiz married Claudina Lazo. During their engagement, every Wednesday and Sunday, he had dutifully swept the patio of Sr. and Sra. Lazo's home. The women generally agreed that the prospective son-in-law's labors represented a fair trade to fill the void left by the daughter, who once married no longer contributed to her parents' home.

Another Lazo family daughter, Petra Lazo, stands among the candles given to "content" her parents.
Ariel Mendoza.

En route to their godparents' home, the author's sister-in-law Adelina walks with her new husband,
Victor, past pre-Hispanic ruins, the colonial Catholic church where they were just married, and
Teotitlán's sacred mountain peak. *Ariel Mendoza.*

Chapter 4

THE WEDDING:
COMING OF AGE

Teotitlán is seldom silent, especially on Wednesdays and Sundays, the days traditionally reserved for weddings. Upbeat marches and dynamite-filled rockets announce to the entire community a wedding procession's itinerary through the village, from the groom's home to the church, from the church to the godparents' home, and back to the home of the groom.

The church ceremony is typically held in the morning; we were married at 8:00 a.m. Our wedding procession departed from the Mendoza home, and Arnulfo and I took our place between his godparents. I was grateful for the walk ahead, a chance to stretch my legs after kneeling before the family altar for the better part of an hour. Teotitecos see the altar as a house of God within each family's home. The words "with God as your witness" ring strong at this paramount moment in the lives of each young couple, kneeling in a haze of incense before such powerful images as Christ crucified and the Virgin of Guadalupe.

Family and friends came forward, one by one, to bestow on us their blessings for a long and happy life together. This brief rite ended when they gently brought our heads to touch, something akin to an affectionate conk. I clearly remember the overwhelming sensation, that indeed I had just been married, when at long length the solemn blessings ended, and Arnulfo and I were signaled to stand. The band's lively marches escorted our wedding party along the four-block promenade to the church.

CHAPTER FOUR

Elaborate baroque rites permeate Catholic religious practices in native Mexico, to such a degree that I often wonder how this could be the same Roman Catholic religion I was raised in. At its best, this symbolism and ritual reinforce profound beliefs and meanings. Examples are the three elements the godparents give to the couple: a lighted candle, a symbol of divine guidance; an intertwining cord that physically joins the couple; and old coins, representing how the groom will support his new wife.

The full brass band climbed to the choir loft, and I couldn't imagine how the tuba player managed to squeeze up three flights of the narrow spiral staircase lugging his massive instrument in hand. The band's sounds boomed and echoed big in the classic acoustics of the eighteenth-century colonial church. The "Diana" signaled the end of the ceremony, and Arnulfo and I emerged to the awaiting crowd. There is no music more inextricably associated with rejoicing than the ubiquitous "Diana," a riotous little tune, an indisputably sonorous exclamation mark. A wheel of firecrackers announced our successfully completed ceremony, the rapid-fire explosions more like the sounds of a western shoot-out than a wedding.

We left the church with Arnulfo's godparents and returned to their home. In a rite steeped in symbolism, as husband and wife we ate the first food of our married life; we shared a tlayuda and atole, the elemental staples of the Zapotec diet. Then the band struck up to escort us back to the Mendoza house, where the fiesta was just gearing up.

꘡꘡꘡

Three fattened pigs were slaughtered the day before Arnulfo and I married on February 15, 1987. Invitados, already hard at work with the preparations, lined up to bless the animals, a combination of praying that the meat be both sufficient and nourishing and giving thanks for their sacrifice.

In a sense, we couldn't get married before Clara had raised these pigs. We also had to wait for Arnulfo's father, Emiliano, to finish his three-year term as appointed mayor of Teotitlán, the most important and time-consuming *cargo*. As the first-born son of a highly respected couple, Arnulfo could only be married in a proper *fandango*—the most elaborate of weddings by Teotitlán standards. A fandango must offer guests two full meals—a breakfast and an afternoon *comida*—include ceremonial dancing with sugar-flower-filled *jicapextles*, and last for two full days.

Only a few decades ago, a bride's wedding gifts would have included not much more than a *baúl* (hope chest), a metate, a few dishes, and, if she were

During the blessing of the gifts, the author sits on a hope chest made by her father.

A selection of *jicapextles* from the author's collection. *Gagnier de Mendoza.*

lucky, a simple armoire. Nowadays, in these economically prosperous times, a bride needs one and sometimes two five-ton trucks to transport her wedding presents from her former home to that of her new in-laws.

Cash is not a common gift. Teotitecos prefer the visual fanfare of tangible presents. When Claudina was married, five months after her engagement, she received no fewer than six china cabinets, seven armoires, several *baules*, two dining room sets, a bed, a sofa set, a refrigerator, a gas range, ten metates, dozens of pots and pans, and hundreds of dishes. Only the bride's family gives gifts, and if we remember the opulent offerings her parents received when Zacarías and Emilia went to content, it is not surprising that an equally lavish display of gifts arrived for the wedding.

Livestock is traditionally given as wedding gifts. *Gagnier de Mendoza.*

Like tender exclamation marks, two dreamy eyed calves, festooned with garlands of huge pink bows, were counted among the presents. They were tethered to a tree in the midst of the hustle and bustle, apparently oblivious to the fiesta commotion. Just yards away, on the other side of the constant foot traffic, a young sow, all done up in her own ribbons, snoozed on the cool, moist earth.

When the gifts had finally been unloaded into the sizable patio, murmurs of amazed approval rippled through the gathering. In due time the huehuete initiated the blessing of the gifts, an impressive and lengthy example of high Zapotec protocol, combining elements of both giving thanks and imploring the divine powers to protect and prolong the useful life of these objects.

At my wedding, several village musclemen were recruited to dance with the gifts. Erasto Gutierrez is renowned for his strength, and he danced with a hope chest my father had made of Canadian hardwood lined with aromatic cedar. Much the way people carry firewood out of the mountains, he fastened both ends of a *mecapal* (tumpline) to the hefty gift, slipped the broad center band around his forehead, and, bending against the weight, heaved my hope chest off the ground. The band started up, and for a good five minutes, Erasto and several other men danced with this and other massive objects. Besides wooden hope chests, Erasto has danced with stone metates and huge china cabinets; he has even danced with refrigerators!

In recent years, with more non-Teotitlán guests attending village weddings, customs have changed. Everyone is invited to gather up their gifts and join in the lively dance. Lots of laughing ensues, as city folks prance about embracing packages of sheets and towels, pots and pans.

In rural Oaxaca, the turkey is synonymous with fiestas. In an amusing counterpoint to the lavish display of wedding presents, the groom's family responds by offering a gift of turkeys to their *consuegros* (the parents of a son-in-law or daughter-in-law; a valued relationship in Teotitlán). This gesture is understood to mean that the big birds will be eaten in *mole amarillo* (yellow mole) the day after the wedding, when the festivities shift to the home of the bride's parents. It isn't good enough to simply hand over the turkeys. In Teotitlán, people adorn the birds with necklaces of fuchsia bougainvillea petals and cigarettes tied to their beaks.

At Claudina's wedding, enveloped in the sounds of the big brass band, Emilia and Zacarías watched with satisfaction as robust young men each gingerly hoisted a live turkey over a shoulder to perform one of the fiesta's most delightful dances. This dance became a street procession as the turkeys, along with bottles of mezcal and a basket of dried chiles, were jigged and bobbed all the way to the home of the new *consuegros,* Braulio and Soledad.

Preparations—the cutting of firewood, the toasting of chiles, and on and on—had begun months in advance. The invitados routinely devote several days to participate in a wedding, helping with the unending cycle of food preparation and joining in the music-filled processions and dancing. In keeping with Teotitlán's code of tradition, such a momentous event as a wedding must be celebrated with corresponding effort and sacrifice.

回回回

Higadito was served for breakfast at our wedding, and Arnulfo drove his mother to all the surrounding village markets the week before to find the five hundred free-range eggs needed for this dish. My mother-in-law couldn't emphasize enough how these eggs, with their rich deep-yellow yolks, were superior to store-bought eggs of suspect quality. Early on the morning of our wedding day, six stately señoras sat on woven *petates* (palm mats), their feet tucked under petticoats and Scotch plaid *enredos* (wrap skirts). Centered before large glazed bowls, they embarked on the task of beating the eggs with the tempered clarity of Zen meditation masters. Minutes ticked by, and while they cut through the viscous amber liquid with their long kitchen knives, five hundred eggs joined in an a cappella fugue of *bulump bulump bulump.*

This egg dish challenges the meaning of capricious, in an instant becoming cantankerous. Local culinary lore is filled with horror stories of important compromisos where the eggs would not coagulate in the broth and simply remained loosely scrambled, never embracing the shredded chicken, never amassing to a firm collected consistency. Could this disaster have been provoked because the young woman who beat the eggs was pregnant? Or could it be that she washed her hands with perfumed soap?

Later in the day, we ate mole negro at our wedding feast. Tía Zenaida had been our *comidera,* and this would be one of her last commissioned jobs—she died several months later. Comideras are Teotitlán's answer to a catering service. These women are experts in preparing vast quantities of food. They can make mole for hundreds and without the aid of written recipes know exactly how much chile and spice are required.

In keeping with village protocol, requesting the services of a comidera involves a rite. Several months before their son's wedding, Antonia and Félix visited Natalia Bautista, affectionately known as Tía Natalia. They were ushered directly to the altar room, and only after lighting a large votive candle and kissing the family altar did they gently enfold the hand of the octogenarian in the traditional greeting of respect, murmuring the word *chxan*. Luck was with them this day; Tía Natalia agreed to be their comidera.

Tía Natalia is one of Teotitlan's senior comideras. Deep-set eyes and the sculpted grooves in her leathery skin speak of her eighty-four years, yet her nimble movements testify that she is an active woman still very much enthused by her craft. In preparation for an upcoming *compromiso*, she might spend hours toasting pound after pound of *guajillo* chiles to delicate perfection. Last year, Arnulfo and I arrived particularly early—at 4:00 a.m.—for a cousin's wedding. Hardly a soul stirred in the large courtyard, but there was Tía Natalia. Still hours before dawn, she had just returned from the *molino* with two massive galvanized tubs, one full of chiles and the other full of herbs and spices.

Tía Natalia, a senior *comidera* in Teotitlán. *Gagnier de Mendoza.*

More than five hundred free-range eggs were used in the *higadito* prepared for the author's wedding. *Gagnier de Mendoza.*

CHAPTER FOUR

Not much more than four foot seven, Tía Natalia is dwarfed by the classic caldron used to cook mole. Each fiesta tests her endurance as she orchestrates the preparation of three or more meals for hundreds of guests. She finds precious little sleep.

I wouldn't do the reader the discourtesy of including the recipe for Teotitlán's *mole negro* (black mole); this dish was never intended for a single person to make in a single session. Mole negro is fiesta food, and it lends itself to preparation in vast quantities, with not only the expertise of a comidera but with many hands to help in the constant stirring of the pot. It is all the more impressive when you admire its glistening jet surface extended over a massive caldron, its sultry aromas hypnotic and intoxicating. No, here I will list only the ingredients, staggering enough in their length:

77 pounds *guajillo* and ancho chiles
154 pounds tomatoes
77 pounds tomatillos
11 pounds raisins
11 pounds sesame seeds
2 pounds almonds
2 pounds pecans
1 pound whole cloves
1/4 pound allspice
1 ginger root
17 bunches thyme
7 bunches Mexican oregano
10 whole nutmegs

Add to taste: chocolate, sugar, finely ground bread crumbs, and home-rendered lard. To all this is added gallons and gallons of rich chicken or turkey stock.

Chocolate atole is reserved for only the most majestic occasions, such as fandangos. Only a handful of village women hold the secrets of preparing the cacao beans for this elusive liquid, and my Tía Natalia, with decades of experience, is one master of this art. At any given moment, she has several caches of beans, all undergoing various stages of anaerobic fermentation, buried in the earth. She nurtures the tiny treasures to maturity, digging them up, rinsing them

Younger women are assigned to making *tlayudas*, the dinner-plate sized corn tortillas favored in Oaxacan villages. *Gagnier de Mendoza.*

off, and burying them again—a process she must repeat several times over several months.

I can't help but wonder how on earth this odd and ancient procedure came about. Cacao beans were once used as money. Did someone protect their precious beans from theft by burying them underground, only to discover this exotic metamorphosis? Or, as the native people believe, was this mysterious knowledge given to them by the gods? This is alchemy, not chemistry.

Once the beans have been dug up and dusted off for the last time, the real labor begins with the peeling of the aged, fragile cacao beans. This painstaking process is achieved with a great deal of patience—and the tip of a straight pin.

Filled with handmade sugar flowers, two *jicapextles* sit atop cases of beer waiting to be danced.

It is more an act of archaeology than gastronomy, as the tiny flakes of the beans' white outer casings fall away like antique lacquer.

For the next step, Tía Natalia works according to ancient tradition, placing a bowl of glowing embers beneath her metate to warm its volcanic stone. Hand grinding the shriveled beans is key to the process, and within seconds they begin to release their natural fat. She blends into this oozing paste a combination of ingredients, all ground and toasted: rice, whole wheat, unfermented cacao beans, and cinnamon, finally forming two-inch-thick patties, which she then scores into cubes and air-dries for several days.

Since I was married in a fandango, I know that chocolate atole was served at my wedding. But to be honest, I was too busy being the bride to remember much of what went on behind the scenes. I do clearly remember its preparation for my brother-in-law Jacobo's wedding in 1995, though. With true production-line efficiency, one row of women leaned over metates, grinding the cubes with a little water, reconstituting them into a thin batter. Like an opposing battalion on a chess board, another row of sisters-in-law, aunts, and cousins knelt over ample bowls of green glazed pottery and, using specially reserved wooden beaters, whipped the batter to a sturdy foam.

They added a little sugar as a final touch, then poured a generous scoop of the buff-colored foam over a bowl of hot corn atole. With a carved wooden stir stick, they blended both mixtures. The result was a rich, warm, sophisticated, and absolutely delicious drink.

回回回

As night enveloped our wedding fiesta, the huehuete, Luis Gutiérrez, resumed his command of the events. To seal new familial bonds created by marriage, the huehuete assigned members from both sides of our family to dance together. He was careful to call a dance that included my new mother-in-law, Clara; my mother, Joan; our wedding godmother; and me, the bride. My mother-in-law invited the *comidera* to dance, to publicly acknowledge her highly imortant role. The band played a *jarabe,* and we danced the quintessential two-step shuffle, not an exuberant display but a dance of ritual solemnity.

An important element that made our wedding a fandango was the dancing with jicapextles, arranged with dozens of fragile white sugar flowers. The flowers are usually supplemented with several pounds of store-bought candies—ballast that anchors the fragile flora in the gourd and ensures that there is plenty of candy to go around. My sisters-in-law were worried that I wouldn't last the lengthy dance under the weight of the hard candies. So to help me out, they

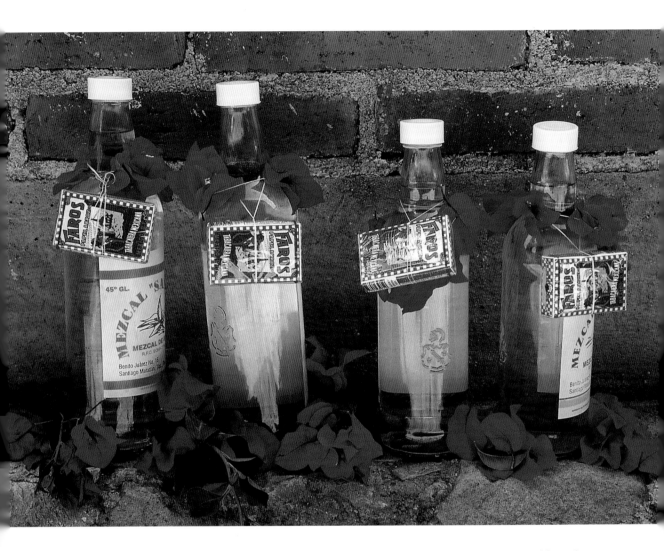

At *fandangos*, men dance with bottles of *mezcal* decorated with bougainvillea and Faros cigarettes.
Ariel Mendoza.

filled the spaces below my showy candy flowers with chocolate-covered marsh-mallows. But I did just fine, at least that's what they said, and for what seemed like forever, and feeling like a horse on short reins, I contained my movements to a semblance of solemnity. When I finished dancing with my godmother and new mother-in-law, Arnulfo carried my jicapextle while I handed out the can-dies, one by one, to all the guests.

Ever attentive to social hierarchy, the huehuete called groups of four or six forward to dance, sometimes mixed couples but often only women or men, and always according to their status. It would be considered an irreparable faux pas to call a lowly second cousin up to dance before the respected godmother had been given her turn. This process unfolded at an unflagging pace, easily tak-ing the better part of five hours before the last guests were called upon to dance.

Unlike many cultures, in which celebration is largely based on participa-tion, the people of Teotitlán seem perfectly content in the role of spectator, some-times dancing only once during the entire night. For the rest of the time they play witness, all the while mingling casual conversation with toasts of mezcal and *tepache* (a lightly fermented beverage), and even the occasional catnap.

The author's wedding. The bride with her husband, Arnulfo, with his sisters and mother.
Ariel Mendoza.

Señoritas bear Our Lady of Sorrows in the Good Friday procession. *Ariel Mendoza.*

Chapter 5

LENT AND HOLY WEEK

ent and Holy Week, more than any other religious fiestas, bring the Catholic deities to the realm of human emotion. These fiestas are charged with associations of loyalty and betrayal, motherly love and mourning, abstinence and indulgence.

The passion plays of Holy Week publicly reenact the crucial events in the last days of the life of Christ, and these events are played out throughout the town. Like the needle on a compass, the massive whitewashed church is the point of departure and return for important processions passing through all five neighborhoods in Teotitlán.

Ash Wednesday marks the beginning of six weeks of penitence. During Lent, women and men commonly make promesas. In exchange for the cleansing of their sins, they abstain from excesses and indulgences such as meat, alcohol, and gambling. As part of the Lenten observances, a statue of Christ carrying the cross departs the church each Friday morning, in a procession that meanders, for just over an hour, through the heart of town.

Not only do the penitents accompany the statue, but the procession dances in a polka-dotted wonder of white chicken-feather and tinfoil angel wings—worn by angelitos dressed in white. The angelitos are living out a slightly different kind of promesa, this time made by their mothers and fathers. Although the angelito's participation is a public act of veneration, there is an underlying belief that, having been an angelito, the child will be protected from illness and accident.

    回回回

On Palm Sunday the church awakens with a change of props. Gone are the elaborately adorned candles that during the rest of the year flank the side altars of the church. In their place stand simple beeswax tapers flying silver cut-paper flags. These somber sentinels stand guard until Christ's ascension to heaven forty days after Easter.

Early this morning, the sacristans lower from its customary niche, on a modest side altar, a statue of Christ—not the solemn image featured during Lent but the jubilant if humble savior riding a donkey. They quietly ferry it to the town's morning food market adjacent to the church. This is where the real event begins. At the entrance to the market, Padre Rómulo blesses massive bundles of palm fronds for the sacristans to distribute after Mass. Reenactments, like storytelling, are both teaching tools and sources of information. In keeping faithful to the Bible, the statue, in the company of the priest, the band, and a strong turnout from the community, makes its own triumphant reentry, as though the gates of the church courtyard were the threshold of Jerusalem.

Shortly after Mass, another drama begins, this time centered on a young man dressed in Roman-style robes. He is playing the role of Pontius Pilate, and it is his duty to gather from every town authority his *bastón de mando* (a staff fashioned from metal or wood and a symbol of governing power). Biblical history places Pontius Pilate as the maximum authority in Roman-ruled Jerusalem, and as such he wields the power to nullify the Municipal Council, even in Teotitlán.

A hot and exhausted *angelito* naps on her father's shoulder during "the encounter." *Ariel Mendoza.*

Holy Monday procession; Teotitecos show their love and devotion with garlands of fresh flowers.
Gagnier de Mendoza.

The little centurion rides his unflappable pony. *Ariel Mendoza.*

Having completed his task, he returns to the church with his arms loaded with staffs, which are bundled together and placed on the main altar until Christ's resurrection on Easter Sunday seven days later.

Village elder Marino Vásquez is quick to point out the irony of Pilate's potent role in Teotitlán, compared to the Bible's decidedly negative portrayal of a man little concerned with saving Christ. Marino explains the symbolism of the act this way: "This is a test and an opportunity to show our goodness to God. We must behave ourselves. There is no one to throw us in jail if we pick a fight and get drunk." Perhaps the dry law enforced throughout the town from Palm Sunday to Easter Sunday aids in this "test of virtue."

回回回

It feels as if the entire village is in some way involved in the dramatic outpouring of faith on Holy Monday, an all-encompassing public enactment, particularly dramatic in Teotitlán. The band leads a procession out of the church at mid-morning, sonorously escorting two nearly life-sized statues. It will be past dark before this event finishes its long loop, winding through the town and back to the church.

Already anticipating the sorrow and grieving that will be hers by the week's end, the Virgin Mary is dressed in black, portraying La Virgen de la Soledad (Our Lady of Solitude), Oaxaca city's patron saint. At her side, Jesus, crowned in thorns, carries a cross. He is still the king on Holy Monday, and here the people greet him and his mother like royalty, offering eggs, ears of dried corn, bouquets of asters, and garlands of blossoms from the delicately perfumed frangipani. With fitting grandeur, the statues are transported on palanquins, each borne on the shoulders of four strong men. Rhythmically swaying to the slow march of the solemn music, the statues appear to be floating upon a sea of shiny, black hair.

Hundreds participate. All ages accompany the procession. Half a dozen little boys dressed up as Roman soldiers escort the statues, while four elders bear black flags and crosses. The Church Committee, the mayor, and his council all represent present-day authority.

A young boy portraying the Roman centurion mounts an amazingly unfazed pony, cloaked from ears to tail in bright ribbons and colorful tin flowers, bells jingling with every step. The centurion is in many ways the *mayordomo* of Holy Week events, and his role as sponsor and host becomes even more apparent on Easter Monday.

The actors pad along engulfed by the faithful, and rowdy young boys scamper in and out, awaiting free tacos and ice cream at the next stop. Napping

Horchata (Rice Milk) with Xiotilla Cactus

The following is adapted from a traditional recipe by Abigail Mendoza. The rice is traditionally ground to a paste on a stone metate, but it can be successfully ground in a blender.

3 cups water
1 cup rice, preferably Mexican medium grain or standard long grain
1 stick cinnamon (preferably Mexican), 2 inches long and 1/2 inch wide, broken in four pieces
2 large ripe red cactus fruits or 6 small native *xiotillas* (substitute 1/2 cup finely diced cantaloupe)
2 1/4 quarts cold water
1 cup sugar or to taste
1 cup toasted pecans, chopped

Soak rice in 3 cups water for 3 hours.
Strain rice and discard water.
In a blender, combine in batches 1/4 cup rice, one of the four cinnamon pieces, and 2 cups cold water. Process from low to high speed.
Pour liquid through a medium-sized strainer into a large jug or small bucket.
Repeat blending process until all rice and cinnamon are ground.
Cut fruit in half and scoop out pulp. Mash pulp with a fork or potato masher.
Mix rice mixture with remaining cold water. Add fruit and sugar.
Add 1 tablespoon chopped pecans to each glass before serving.

Serve with a spoon. Makes 10 glasses.

Refreshing *nieves* cool the body and emotions after the heat and intensity of Holy Week. *Gagnier de Mendoza.*

angelitos dot the procession, heads limp, heavy on their mothers' shoulders. Whole families have turned out for this outing, and fathers armed with video cameras document its progress. Once again the line blurs between the actors and the audience.

Twelve stops are scheduled for Mary and Jesus at designated places along the main streets of town. Groups of neighbors surrounding these stops erect *casitas*— momentary "homes" for the statues—made from metal frames with the neighbors' own handwoven rugs forming walls and roofs. Until about thirty years ago, elders remember the casitas were made of *petates*—mats woven from a native palm. Then year after year, more groups opted to lend handwoven rugs to the event, until eventually the use of rugs became a tradition. The rugs' complicated Aztec calendar design is vivid in my husband Arnulfo's childhood memories. He recalls how the men in his neighborhood would weave night and day to finish a large rug in time for the Holy Monday procession. The economic pulsebeat of Teotitlán flows through its rug sales, and to shade and protect their most revered deities with the very objects that sustain the life and welfare of the community is an act of gratitude to God.

Temperatures soar during Holy Week, and by mid-afternoon the procession advances under an intense heat. María Luisa carries little Jacobo, a sturdy angelito about to turn three. Beads of sweat trickle down the hairline of both mother and son, and I marvel that no one has fainted from heatstroke. In a heartening gesture of group effort, sustenance awaits the penitents at each stop. The residents neighboring each of the twelve casitas have agreed among themselves to offer refreshments to the procession. At the sixth stop, on the main street through town, the Mendoza Ruiz family has been busy for hours, preparing vegetable tacos and *horchata* (fresh rice milk) for the imminent arrival of the twohundred-plus penitents they plan on feeding. I know this because I am assigned to the crumbled-cheese-sprinkling station on the taco production line. A few feet away, my sister-in-law Rosario fills hundreds of heavy ten-ounce glasses with the cool, sweet drink. The glasses have been resurrected from a former life, when they housed slow-burning votive candles on the family altar—testimony to decades of faith. The neighbors across the street will distribute *nieves*, or sorbets, literally translated as "snow." Twelve wooden barrels lined with rock salt and ice hold steel cylinders brimming with *nieves* in three traditional flavors: *tuna* (red cactus fruit), *leche quemada* (burnt milk), and lime. Underscoring the idiosyncrasy of Mexican patriotism, it is no coincidence that the red, white, and green *nieves* echo the colors of Mexico's flag. With astonishing order and organization, within thirty minutes more than two hundred people have been refueled, rehydrated, and refreshed, ready to proceed a few more blocks to the next casita.

Elders play the roles of the twelve apostles for the Holy Thursday Last Supper. *Ariel Mendoza.*

Traditions are malleable, adapting to changing times. Just as the former palm mat casitas are now made from woven rugs, other changes have occurred in Teotitlán's Holy Monday procession. Going back only a few decades, *tejate* was the standard refreshment passed out during the procession. In 2001, in a bid to keep a tenuous hold on old tradition, *tejate* was served but only once. Present-day bellies are better filled along the way with tacos, tamales, thirst-quenching fruit water, and *nieves*.

At 11:00 a.m. on Holy Thursday, Mass is celebrated followed by the reenactment of the Last Supper. The church allows for some fudging on the details, and Teotitlán hosts not a supper but a last *comida*, eaten at midday. The same statue of Christ that was central to the Holy Monday procession is now clothed in a golden vestment; the cross has been removed, and symbolic of the bread and wine shared at the Last Supper, a chalice and a large *pan de yema* (rich Oaxaca egg bread) have been tied to the statue's hands. Far from simply administering rites, the presiding priest plays a leading role in this publicly staged theater, seated at the opposite end of the table from Christ's statue and flanked on either side by the twelve apostles.

Traditional cultures are often perceived as static and unchanging, when in fact change slips in and out in this fertile, continually evolving environment, oscillating back and forth between old and new. For innumerable generations, twelve respected elders—each one distinguished as an apostle by a monogrammed satin sash, slung from the shoulder in beauty-contest fashion—were selected for the reenactment, but in 2001 young men played the roles of the apostles. Unlike the elders, all were catechism teachers, well versed in reciting the event's lengthy prayers. The following year, the elders were back with their ribbons and laurel wreaths and above all their much-respected presence.

Two members of the Church Committee called *cobradores* are in charge of collecting established quotas to cover the cost of candles for the church, fireworks for fiestas, and general church maintenance. The *cobradores* also collect quotas from each married couple to cover the cost of Holy Week festivities; couples paid seventy pesos each in 2004. In keeping with the *cargo* system, whereby unpaid, obligatory positions usually entail personal expenditure, the *cobradores* are personally responsible for covering the expenses of the Last Supper. In typical Teotitlán grandeur, this meal is abundant. As is the custom, the *cobradores* and their wives call upon the help of family, including brothers, sisters, and compadres, to form an impressive matrix of efficiency. The women prepare the food,

During the Holy Monday procession, the statues of Christ and the Virgin are protected by walls of rugs loaned for the occasion by weavers neighboring each of the twelve stations. *Gagnier de Mendoza.*

while the men serve it. First, each member of the Last Supper receives a platter heaped with sweet breads and a cup of chocolate. Then they eat the main dish—batter-fried salted fish and white beans in a garlic cumin broth, garnished with chiles and tomatoes. The meal ends with a quarter of a watermelon and a bunch of plantains. As is customary in Teotitlán, the enormous portions will be taken home to share with family. This meal is served at several sittings, and no sooner do the apostles leave the table than the Church Committee sits down to eat, only to be followed by the town authorities. Lastly the *cobradores* and their support group will finally eat, nearly four hours after the event began.

The mood of Holy Thursday intensifies with the evening's rituals. Following the celebration of the liturgy within the church, the procession of the holy monstrance begins. The monstrance contains a consecrated Host called the Santísimo, meaning "the holiest of the holy," and the ritual begins as the priest lowers the sunburst-shaped monstrance from its place within the tabernacle. The procession departs the church, along with the priest bearing the monstrance; both are protected by a large purple canopy, each corner sustained by a member

The priest is protected beneath a canopy in a procession of church and municipal authorities. *Ariel Mendoza.*

of the Church Committee. Heading up the procession, the *síndico* (second to the mayor in authority) holds a large lacquered gourd, while the mayor sprinkles its contents of bougainvillea blossoms and grapefruit leaves in front of the path of the priest. The retinue is closed by the president and vice president of the Church Committee. Both hold candelabras of seven tapers, believed in Teotitlán to represent each of the seven Holy Sacraments. This scene is accompanied by a brass band, a drum, and the wailing *chirimía*. Everyone circumambulates the courtyard of the church, finalizing the full circuit by returning to the main altar. To encourage the congregation to visit, the doors of the church remain open throughout the night. This is the only night of the year when the tabernacle's doors are left open and the monstrance containing the consecrated Eucharistic bread is removed and exhibited. To guarantee a continuous vigil with hymns, chants, and prayers, specific hours are assigned to different age groups and town councils. While the señoritas of Teotitlán are given the safe and decent daylight hour of 6:00 to 7:00 a.m. to keep vigil, the municipal authorities are expected to do their part at three o'clock in the morning.

By Teotitlán standards, the scene on the altar is downright minimalist: simple candles, white lilies, the bundle of staffs, and the monstrance. In a parallel reality not far away, another scene rich in pre-Hispanic/Christian syncretism unfolds. We are witnesses of Christ's incarceration. In the northern corner of the church's patio, a small covered archway is transformed into a symbolic jail cell. Shortly after dark, the statue of Christ is led from the church accompanied by the centurion on horseback, the twelve apostles, the thirteen members of the Church Committee, and what seems to be the entire village population. Noticeably absent at this event is the priest, for whom this tradition is decidedly too "folkloric," void of ecclesiastical validity. Christ is placed inside the barely twelve-foot-square chamber, where he will spend the night. For the people of Teotitlán, their visitation to the statue is an essential act of veneration, and they come to accompany the Lord during his long night of suffering. Entire families wait patiently in line, for an hour or more, to visit the jailed Christ. The line of waiting faithful is separated from the statue by a *petate*, and one by one, small groups are ushered behind the straw mat curtain to pay their respects. After kneeling before Christ and invoking a brief silent prayer, the faithful leave coins on the collection tray and in turn receive from the attending members of the Church Committee a stem or two of blessed flowers. In absolute faith, women rub these consecrated blooms over the bodies of their husbands and children, giving them the ultimate in protection.

The Catholic Church walks a fragile tightrope between enforcing official doctrine and tolerating indigenous idolatry. It is essential to understand that for

Christ, Our Lady of Sorrows, Mary Magdalene, and Saint John are returned to the church after the Good Friday "encounter." *Ariel Mendoza.*

95

much of the native population, there is no difference between Christ, the Virgin, and the saints or their statues. Kissing the carved wooden feet of a statue of Christ is to kiss God himself.

回回回

By 10:00 a.m. on Good Friday, the civic plaza is filling. Vendors, their baskets filled with popcorn, *tortas*, and clay pots of *nixuatole* (a gelatinous dessert made from fresh cornstarch—cheap and really quite palatable), have staked out cool spots under the few shade trees.

Suffering through the midday sun is the real essence of the event. One *should* suffer, for the scene about to unfold teaches the greatest suffering of all. Just hours ago, the statue of Christ carrying the cross was removed from its jail cell and lifted to an awaiting palanquin. With the first solemn notes of the band, the statue commenced its lonely procession, winding through the lanes behind the church before entering the plaza through a narrow passageway beside the town hall.

The Virgin Mary, Mary Magdalene, and Saint John lead a parallel procession, accompanied by another band that slowly advances from the church, through the streets, in the opposite direction of Christ. Each band plays a different dirge, and the dissonance of the two distinct melodies creates an escalating tension, as both processions near the plaza. The moment is suspended in a calculated cacophony. The entire happening is made all the more acute because everyone knows what is to come; yet at exactly what instant it will take place remains uncertain.

Finally, the Virgin Mary appears, parting the crowd as she enters the esplanade. The bearers inch her closer and closer to her son, until finally they are face to face. This is *el encuentro* ("the encounter"), the emotional last moment mother and son have together. The statues are tilted. Their heads touch in a symbolic final embrace. The amplified voice of the priest jolts us back to reality, and from an impromptu pulpit, in a larger version of a Holy Monday tent of rugs, he delivers a sermon focused on the pain of a mother before the death of her son.

An intermission of sorts ensues; the statues are ushered into the dark coolness of the church, while Teotitecos break for a refreshing *nieve*. More than a dozen stalls have been set up to accommodate hundreds of customers, all hot and thirsty. The villagers return to their homes for a meatless meal of salted fish and white beans or chile rellenos.

By late afternoon another powerful drama unfolds within the church. The altar is the stage, and the priest and the statue of Christ are the principal play-

For "the encounter," vendors in the adjacent artesans market lend their rugs to enclose the pulpit.
Ariel Mendoza.

ers, while the congregation not only bears witness to the unfolding events but participates in them.

Mass begins with the reading of several psalms, followed by the priest's commentaries. The biblical references, primarily taken from the Gospels, unfold in a sequential order leading up to the actual Crucifixion. Like theater in the round, the statue of Christ on the cross emerges from the entrance to the church. All heads turn to witness the mysterious figure, completely concealed within lengths of white cotton, held high by a solemn sacristan, who proceeds to the altar with slow measured steps and delivers his charge into the care of the priest. Over the next quarter hour, we experience the unveiling of Christ. First one arm is uncovered by the priest, then the other, followed by the feet and lastly the entire torso. Each movement is punctuated by a prayer. The sacristans unroll a knotted pseudo-Persian carpet on the steps leading to the main altar and with profound reverence gently lay upon it the figure of the crucified Christ. Only now is the congregation allowed to advance. In four raggedy lines, the faithful patiently await their turn to kneel, some fully prostrating themselves upon the floor, for the fleeting instant to kiss their God.

By now it is 7:00 p.m., and the church has filled to the point of bursting. There is barely enough room to shift from one foot to another, and a stifling humidity has replaced the great chamber's typical coolness. The mood is heavy. Inertia seems to detain time. So painfully near the end of their Lenten promesa, sweaty angelitos lie limp on their mothers' shoulders, suspended in lethargic comas.

The solemn Mass of the Crucifixion officially ends almost three hours after it began. The priest, having finished with his contracted duties, climbs into his car and drives away. At this twilight hour, the following chain of events belongs solely to the people; these are rituals removed from the official Catholic Church. With a brief intermission, the scenery changes, and a massive purple curtain concealing the main altar is pulled back to reveal a twenty-foot cross with a life-sized Christ nailed to it. Four men wearing white robes and white gloves appear before the altar and lean two wooden ladders against the cross.

Although their name, *los varones*, simply means "the men," they belong to a respected lineage. Domingo Gutiérrez explains how the *varones* represent Joseph of Arimathea and Nicodemus, who in the Gospel according to John lowered Jesus from the cross and placed him in the tomb. Early Franciscan and Dominican missionaries, faced with native-speaking congregations, used this kind of representational participation to evangelize. Marino Vásquez confirms popular memory when he recalls how years ago, the *varones* were elders, men of merit, worthy of touching Christ. Over time this earned position became an inherited one, and the young men now ascending the ladders to Christ are the sons and grandsons of those respected elders.

On one ladder, a *varon* removes the wooden nail from Christ's right hand. The statue has articulated shoulder joints, and the arm is gently lowered to its side. Then the *varón* on the other ladder lowers the left arm in a similar manner. Yet another *varón* removes the nail in Christ's foot, and finally the length of muslin holding Christ to the cross is loosened, and the statue slips gently into the awaiting arms of the last *varón*. In a series of what appear to be well-rehearsed maneuvers, they lower the not only life-sized but very lifelike body of Christ into his tomb, a magnificent carved and gilded coffin complete with windows for public viewing.

Before the priest left he offered a parting word of advice. He reminded the villagers that the statue of Saint Peter has no place in accompanying the body of Christ to the cemetery—that in fact this apostle denied Christ on three occasions, was absent throughout the Lord's suffering, and did not reappear until after the resurrection on Easter Sunday. In short, "Get the story straight." Tradition-entrenched Teotitlán tends to do things as it sees fit, and San Pedro, the father of the church, clutching his keys, is made ready for the procession just as he has been since time immemorial.

Christ's coffin. *Ariel Mendoza.*

CHAPTER FIVE

Black-cloaked *encapuchados,* like hooded monks, emerge from the sacristy and slow-shuffle the length of the main nave before exiting the church; each one carries a different symbol of Christ's stigmata: A locally carved red wooden rooster represents Peter's betrayal of Christ "three times before the cock would crow." The nails removed from the cross rest in one lacquered jicapextle, and in another is nestled Christ's crown of thorns. Another *encapuchado* carries the spear that pierced Christ's heart, and the fifth one sustains Teotitlán's own Shroud of Turin, painted by my husband, artist Arnulfo Mendoza. The *encapuchados* and four men carrying the statue of San Pedro officially escort the entombed Christ to the cemetery, followed by a crowd of more than a hundred men, women, and children.

Shortly after, a parallel procession slowly advances from the church. It is comprised of the Virgin Mary, Saint John, and Mary Magdalene, the same supportive trio that starred in "the encounter" earlier in the day. Just twelve hours before, the mother of Jesus was represented by the statue of La Virgen de los Dolores (Our Lady of Sorrows). Now, after Christ's Crucifixion, she is depicted in mourning, dressed in black as La Virgen de la Soledad. Symbolic of his burial, these nearly life-sized statues once again "encounter" Christ in the cemetery, where the procession circumambulates the graveyard accompanied by the plaintive tones of the band and the emotionally stirring wails of the alabanceros. The day's events draw to a close when the two processions, now united, return to the church. The five statues will stand guard down the center aisle of the main nave for the next forty days, and only after Ascension Day will they be returned to their niches along the side altars.

౷౷౷

A tour of the town on Holy Saturday would find dozens of new wells—all done up like Easter bonnets with brilliant bougainvillea blossoms—awaiting the blessing of their water. On the rocky foothills of the northern Sierra Madre, water is a near-constant concern, especially during Lent and Easter, the driest time of year. Most Teotitecos drink high-quality spring water tapped at its source, in the mountains above the town, yet many people still bring a jug of water from their wells to be blessed by the priest.

౷౷౷

A curious event takes place on Easter Sunday. A small statue (by Teotitlán standards), locally referred to as *San Saración,* is removed from the church.

Everyone agrees that the statue is of Christ, yet no one I asked knew quite why it was called San Saración. Unraveling a linguistic riddle, Teotitecos Arnulfo and Tito Mendoza conjecture that the statue was originally called Christ of the Resurrection but that hundreds of years ago, when the statue arrived, the word *resurrección* was very difficult for the entirely Zapotec-speaking population to pronounce. So natives baptized it with the "Zapotecized" name *Saración*.

The Christ of the Resurrection spends the better part of the morning perched atop his palanquin, facing the village food market just beyond the gates of the churchyard. Floral arches of bougainvillea and marigolds protect the statue from the intense sun. There it remains, receiving flowers, coins, and kisses from Teotitlán's señoras as they return from market, their sturdy baskets laden with chicken, pork, or beef. They believe that the statue's gaze imparts a blessing for their food, and after days and in some cases weeks of abstention, today's aromas of rich meat dishes tantalize eager bellies. Easter Sunday provides a transition zone from Holy Week piety to the revelry of the Danza de los Viejos, a unique post-Easter carnival just one day away.

Tía Reyna visits the statues of Christ and his mother
on Holy Monday. *Gagnier de Mendoza.*

The masked *viejo* with his "wife," a man dressed in native costume. *Gagnier de Mendoza.*

Chapter 6

POST-EASTER REVELRY: LA DANZA DE LOS VIEJOS

T he *Danza de los Viejos (Dance of the Elders)* begins on Easter Monday. But who are these two masked elders? According to eighty-two-year-old Abraham Mendoza Vásquez, *viejo* for his neighborhood for nearly thirty years, "They are the spirits of the dead. They are the village elders who have died and returned, resurrected just like Christ. That is why they appear after Easter Sunday."

The two viejos speak to the community, including the municipal authorities, as if they were their children. In the role of *el viejo mayor,* the principal elder introduces the *viejo menor* as a youngster of a mere one hundred years—the *viejo mayor* being a full fifty years older. They tell their tale of life's long journey, of the mistakes they have made by being impetuous and headstrong. They have returned to give hard-learned advice and hopefully save their sons from making the same mistakes.

After forty-five days of Lenten penitence and Holy Week abstinence, this fiesta comes as a great relief to everyone. It is time to strike up the band, kick up your heels, and let the revelry commence.

Teotitlán is divided into five *secciones* (neighborhoods), and each one hosts the carnival for a single day. In contrast to familial fiestas such as weddings and baptisms, this celebration brings unrelated neighbors in each *sección* together. Around the neighborhood, the fiesta rotates from house to house. Perfecto Lazo and his wife, Meche Montaño, had volunteered to host the fiesta in their home, and 2004 was the last year of their three-year term. Before that, my mother-in-law

The mask of the *viejo* has movable jaws. *Gagnier de Mendoza.*

had been the hostess. To finance the event, each *sección* forms a committee, with a president, secretary, treasurer, and voting members, all usually diehard Danza de los Viejos enthusiasts. They seek out voluntary contributions for the fiesta, knocking on each door of their *sección*. Precise bookkeeping is expected of the treasurer, who will render accounts to the committee, detailing who gave donations in cash or in kind. Chickens, beer, and corn are all quite acceptable contributions.

Omecio Lazo Contreras, a man of sixty-one, stands before the altar in the home of Perfecto and Meche. Omecio has the undivided attention of the two masked viejos, who listen intently to his words of experience. So they should, since Omecio played the role of *viejo mayor* for more than forty years and is coaching the new viejos in the nuances of the lengthy monologues they are expected to deliver in just a few hours. The viejos represent old Zapotecs, and as such speak only in Zapotec, careful not to mix in many Spanish words.

Omecio feels the dancers' masks take on power over time, and more than a decade may pass before a new mask is commissioned. He confesses his difficulty in taking on the role of the viejo without the aid of his mask: "The words don't

Several "generations" of masks hang from a loom at Perfecto Lazo's home. *Gagnier de Mendoza.*

come to me without it." Abraham adds his feelings about the mask. "Very hot and stooped over for long hours, I would feel old, like a real viejo. I would forget who I was and become the viejo," he explains in Zapotec. The mask's movable jaws further enhance its mystique, and a wire apparatus secured within allows the viejo to move the jaws in sync with his speaking. The viejo can even open the mask's mouth wide enough to throw back the occasional shot of mezcal.

Both the viejos are accompanied by male dancers portraying their wives, affectionately known to the community as *naans,* the Zapotec word for "grandmother." Although a *naan* says little throughout the twelve-hour performance, her role is essential; like canned laughter on a sitcom, her cackles explode as exclamation marks right on the heels of the viejo's ribald jokes, infecting the public with uncontrollable laughter. Time and again I have been told that Zapotec jokes just don't have the same humor when translated into Spanish.

Joel plays the role of the senior *naan* and along with his junior counterpart seeks the expertise of the older women. Macaria Ruiz, immaculately dressed in a traditional wool plaid wrap cinched with a fuchsia *faja* (sash), thick satin ribbons braided into her salt-and-pepper hair, stands intently before Joel as she deftly pleats his cochineal-dyed *enredo,* tucks in his embroidered blouse, knots just so the bright pink silk sash, and arranges over his shoulder the folds of his indigo shawl. He wedges his feet into ladies' huaraches and secures a wig braided with satin ribbons upon his head. Up to this point, Joel's costume is a perfect replica of the traditional ceremonial dress used by Teotitlán women half a century before.

It is late afternoon, and dozens of neighbors have been together at the fiesta since early morning. For the main meal, the women have prepared *mole amarillo,* its sturdy russet sauce heady with the enigmatic root beer–like flavor of *hierba santa,* along with the milder flavors of *guajillo* and ancho chiles. Needless to say, the band is settled in, and the festive mood has already been firmly established with several rounds of dances. The viejos and their "wives" emerge from a neighboring home through a lush footpath, and in true ceremonial custom begin their visit at the altar room at Perfecto and Meche's home. The stooped viejos grunt, and all the neighbors respectfully greet these honored guests, lowering their gaze and muttering *chxan.* These new viejos have learned their roles well.

In a town that exults in parades and processions, not a beat is missed as the viejos and their enthusiastic entourage are accompanied to the town plaza with the cymbal crashes and trumpet blasts of the indispensable brass band. The viejos greet the mayor and his council in high ceremonial Zapotec, and in an act packed with symbolism, the viejos lay down their *bastones* on the mayor's table,

Elders play the roles of the twelve apostles for the Holy Thursday Last Supper. The two *viejos* and their "wives" pose with the neighbors of *sección primera*. The author's husband is at far right.
Gagnier de Mendoza.

in effect assuming the governing powers of the village during the next couple
hours of their visit. A village so respectful of hierarchy, Teotitlán views its mayor
as the maximum secular authority, essentially removed from open public criti-
cism. Yet the viejos, with their "otherworldly" nature, are freed from the laws of
the living. Since they are seen as the ancestors of each and every villager, it is
not only their privilege but also their duty to call attention to political shortcom-
ings, administrative oversights, shoddy public works, and outright embezzling.
According to the locals, the mayor greets the viejos with a certain amount of
trepidation, aided and abetted by his own conscience, wary of the reproaches he
might receive in public. The viejos can go so far as to bring up illicit romances
and other social improprieties. After the ceremonial exchanges have concluded
in the confines of the inner chambers, the viejos invite the mayor and his council to dance in the public plaza.

    Hundreds of villagers have gathered by now, entire families converging on
the plaza, all anxious to be entertained. This is where the community's most
relaxed fiesta begins, in its own version of a costume ball. Dozens of Teotitecos
show up, some dressed as women, others as grotesque monsters, the occasional
gorilla, and every now and then a bride and groom. Regardless of the costume's
gender, only men participate, their true identities well concealed behind masks
of wood, rubber, or papier-mâché. Some even attend in risqué outfits—teased
wigs, stuffed bosoms, and high-heeled shoes—but by dramatic contrast others
arrive in the traditional dress of older women: embroidered blouses, *enredos*, and
black woolen braids crisscrossed by satin ribbons.

    A few hours after dark, the improvised open-air fiesta departs the plaza
headed toward the home of the centurion, the living link between the events of
Holy Week and these festivities. In many respects, the centurion is the *mayordomo*, hosting nightly fiestas during the five days the viejos are in town. The
young boy portraying the Roman centurion is seldom more than twelve, so in
reality this major compromiso is assumed by his parents, sometimes to fulfill a
promesa or to accrue spiritual and social merit. Any way you look at it, this compromiso is a marathon.

    Upon entering the home of the centurion, the viejos, *naans*, and senior
men from the *sección* all proceed directly to "visit" the altar. The viejos greet the
centurion with an embrace and a gift—ranging from a live lamb to school sup-
plies. The little centurion, his parents, and their immediate and extended family
all assemble to hear the viejos' words. Speaking before the family altar—the
equivalent of a direct connection to God—the *viejo mayor* emphasizes the purpose of their visit: to celebrate the resurrection of Christ.

A *viejo* shuffles and rocks at a dance in the municipal plaza. *Ariel Mendoza.*

The *viejo mayor* dances with the mayor of Teotitlán in the municipal plaza.

With the formalities over, the viejos invite everyone to gather in the patio, where the dancing begins. As important as the viejos are, they do not partake of the very first dance. The two *naans* are dance partners to the young centurion and his father; only after they dance do the two viejos dance, paired with the centurion's mother and whenever possible his godmother. This part of the fiesta, celebrated in the home of the centurion, provides a parenthesis in the community's highly codified social norms. It is one of the few occasions when everyone—provided they come in costume—is welcomed into a private home. After the first ritual dances are observed, anyone and everyone can join in. A saying goes that on this night, "Bailen hasta los mocosos" ("Even runny-nosed kids can join the dance").

In the course of the night, a special variation of *tepache* is poured from huge jugs of green glazed pottery and served to the guests in simple hollow gourds. No Teotitlán fiesta would be complete without *pan dulce* and hot chocolate served along with *tortas* or tamales to fortify the guests and keep them dancing until the band plays its last *jarabe* sometime around 3:00 a.m.

Even a modest Teotitlán celebration seems extravagant by city standards, yet the centurion's family deserves a special award for their stamina; for five nights running, they repeat this event as the viejos and accompanying representatives from each neighborhood are danced and dined till the wee hours of the morning.

The author and her husband with both *viejos*. Note her apron. *Gagnier de Mendoza.*

The mask of the *viejo* has movable jaws. *Gagnier de Mendoza.*

Hundreds of señoritas wait for the signal to begin the *convite. Ariel Mendoza.*

Chapter 7

DANCING FOR THE GODS: CELEBRATING THE PATRON SAINTS

Teotitlán is populated with a pantheon of saints, filled with mind-boggling manifestations of the Virgin Mary, and guardian to a host of Christ figures: Christ in a coffin, Christ riding a burro, and one whose specialty is blessing the meat. They are all celebrated, with varying degrees of opulence, whether on intimate altars or in grand processions.

Every home keeps a private family altar. Some are simple arrangements sparse with icons, but other altars have become testimonies to generations of devotion. Such is the case with the altar in the home of my uncle and aunt, Agustín Ruiz and his wife, Reyna Gutiérrez. They are the second-generation keepers of the beloved statue of San Isidro Labrador, the patron saint of farmers, always accompanied by a pair of yoked oxen.

Although Tío Agustín makes his living from weaving, he is inextricably connected with the earth. I can hear the cadence in his voice quicken when he speaks about *el campo*, about working the fields. The carved wooden image of San Isidro Labrador holds a very special place in the hearts of the extended Ruiz family because Agustín's father (and my husband Arnulfo's grandfather), Antonio Ruiz Carreño, brought this santo back from his pilgrimage to Esquipulas, Guatemala, in 1923.

Each year for San Isidro's feast, Agustín and Reyna hire a full brass band. The twenty or so musicians arrive late on the evening of May 14. Until well past midnight, they direct their sonorous tribute to the diminutive santo, with stirring clarinet solos and booming baritone bass lines. Marches, waltzes, and *danzones* ring past the walled patio, blanketing the village in familiar melody. All through the evening and again the next day, extended family come to visit the image, offering elegant gladiolas or garlands made from pungent jasmine blossoms fresh picked from their gardens. They kiss the altar, light votive candles, and kneel, invoking a brief silent prayer. *Copitas* (shot glasses) of mezcal —toasts to San Isidro and testimony to sustaining community—make the rounds late into the night. By Teotitlán standards, this is an intimate family gathering, but the Ruiz family is prodigious; Reyna calculates they have prepared fifty gallons of *mole de Castillo* (see page 146) for the feast of honor.

The counterparts of this kind of family compromiso are the grand public fiestas honoring the church's principal patron saints. These beloved deities attract long lines of the faithful, who patiently await their turn. One of my earliest memories of being part of the Mendoza family, and by extension a member of the community, involves standing in line, in the delicious coolness of the church, surrounded by my mother-in-law and troupe of sisters-in-law, all of them still unmarried. It must have been September 8, because when finally we had advanced to the head of the line, it was the Virgin of the Nativity who stood before us. We were each given a coin to drop in the collection tray. We all invoked a short prayer silently, then my mother-in-law extracted a fresh gladiola from the dozens jammed in the vases flanking either side of the statue. Ever so lightly, she brushed the flower over the Virgin's brocaded gown, by which it absorbed the powers of the divine. In turn, she brushed the consecrated stem over our bodies, protecting us from both malevolence and malady. She performed this rite with infinite conviction, just as her mother and grandmother had done unto her on countless occasions in her distant past.

回回回

By July the rains have come to Teotitlán. The crops have been planted, but a vast chasm exists between the fragile seedlings and a successful harvest. Luck is not enough: the favor of the gods is essential.

Second-generation danzante Manuel Ruiz Martínez speaks for his community when he explains, "Going far back to our ancestors, we have danced to venerate the gods, and if we don't, they become sad." In 1580, less than sixty years after Dominican friars began evangelizing in Teotitlán, the Spanish colonial tax collector Gaspar Asensio wrote, "They have the custom of dancing before their gods, throughout the night they dance in their own particular style elated by spirited libations." This same text could be well applied to the fiestas honoring the Catholic deities in contemporary Teotitlán.

The official patroness of the village is the Virgin of the Nativity, and her statue occupies center stage on the main altarpiece of the church. However, the majestic painting *La Preciosa Sangre* (The Precious Blood of Christ)—in Teotitlán endowed with near-miraculous powers—has the greater stature. The painting, ten by six feet, resides in the northern niche of the church, closest to the main altar. This major canvas is attributed to the seventeenth-century school of Miguel Cabrera, a renowned native painter of colonial Oaxaca.

Marino Ruiz Vásquez tells a popular story believed by many: "Hundreds of years ago, the village priest had a maid, and the maid had a child. One day the mischievous boy climbed up on the altar below the painting of the *Preciosa Sangre*, tipped over an oil lamp, igniting the altar cloth, and was burned to death. The village took this as a sign from God that greater reverence must be shown for the powerful image, and from that remote moment, the icon has been venerated with fervor and commitment."

The power of the composition emanates from the crucified Christ. A virtual wellspring of blood pours from his heart, nearly filling a chalice of oversized dimensions. A diaphanous triad contains the head of Christ, the archetypal image of God the Father, and the Holy Spirit in the form of a dove. A celestial battle in the eastern sky depicts a swashbuckling archangel Saint Michael overpowering the devil. The canvas is magnificently framed with a carved wooden vine, echoing the grapevine entwining the crucifix, further reinforcing the association between sacrificial blood and agricultural plenty.

By the 1970s, the painting's visual iconography was virtually obliterated by years of deterioration caused by humidity and mold. In 1982 Arnulfo's parents and Silvestre and Catarina Vicente became the *mayordomos* of the *Preciosa Sangre*, whereby they were responsible for monthly fiestas honoring the patron saints. Arnulfo was studying art at the Escuela de Bellas Artes in Oaxaca, and he and his father convinced the Church Committee to allow them to restore the painting as an act of devotion. For the first time in centuries, the painting was lowered from its loft. On the floor of the main nave, under the guidance of restoration professor Primitivo García, Arnulfo and a team of village men tackled the complex process of rehydrating the oil paint, removing the mold, and stabilizing the image. The Church Committee and Town Council instigated twenty-four-hour vigils during the restoration, and special rosaries were organized in the evenings to pray for the fast and complete convalescence of the beloved image. Concerned and loyal villagers came daily, making offerings of fresh flowers and votive candles. When the restoration was complete, a jubilant congregation turned out for a day of celebration, and the danzantes offered their spirited steps to their glorious *Preciosa Sangre*. The reincarnated canvas, now permanently protected behind glass, glows with the effusive imagery central to classic Mexican baroque painting.

回回回

Up until the nineteenth century, Teotitlán was the equivalent of the county seat, an importance that reflects its veiled but glorious pre-Hispanic past. Teotiteco Domingo Gutiérrez is a grassroots historian of village tradition. He explains, "The first missionaries did not assign to Teotitlán a simple saint as patron, but gave it no less than the duo of the son of God, embodied in *The Precious Blood of Christ,* and his mother, Mary, manifested here as the Virgin of the Nativity."

The preeminence given to the Fiesta of the Precious Blood of Christ is confirmed by a repetition of the celebrations on the *octava.* That is, events occurring on Monday, Tuesday, and Wednesday are repeated again on Friday, Saturday, and Sunday. The principal day of this festival cycle oscillates between the first and second Wednesday of July, drawing the faithful and curious from the farthest reaches of the valley. Each year the Church Committee prints a poster announcing the events, a broadside reaching oversized proportions and an enduring testimony to the fiesta's grandeur.

回回回

The fair comes to Teotitlán but once a year, rolling into town in the first days of July as part of the fiesta. Ramshackle mechanical rides invade the public basketball court, and games of chance strangle the municipal food market. Daily routine is exchanged for fiesta time, as entire families, commonly three generations strong, peruse the fairgrounds. Food concessions proffering fried plantains slathered with sweetened condensed milk, or young field corn topped with mayonnaise, chile powder, and lime juice, do a brisk business with the late evening crowd.

Children are giddy with the excitement of the fair. They ride battered fiberglass jeeps, trucks, and trains, coursing over minute tracks animated by terrifying electrical connections. My niece Silvia, pristine in a new dress and shiny patent leather shoes, swings from the hands of her mother, María Luisa, and her aunt Rufina. My son, Gabriel, and nephew Emiliano are among the packs of rambunctious boys racing through the fair, deciding how best to spend their peso allowances. After much deliberation, they try their luck at throwing darts to burst balloons, winning cheap plastic toys or plaster piggy banks.

Religious standards traditionally are made from dyed sawdust and dried flowers. *Ariel Mendoza.*

Only girls carry adorned baskets but boys joust their homemade figures. Left to right: The author's son, Gabriel, and his cousins Emiliano and Julián. *Gagnier de Mendoza.*

The Mendoza sisters with their nieces, dressed for the *convite. Ariel Mendoza.*

We all play rounds of *la lotería* (Mexico's pictorial version of bingo), giving our full attention to the caller, who announces each card with rhyming verse and double entendres. The tension rises as markers made from dried corn kernels accumulate on the boards until someone yells "Lotería!" That someone was me in 1997. I had filled my entire card! The caller confirmed the win with a playback, bellowing card names like the Nopal Cactus, the Heart, the Skeleton, and the Devil. As the crowd geared up for the next round, exchanging stale boards for more auspicious icons, I, as the winner, chose from fantastically utilitarian prizes such as buckets, wash basins, and enamel pots. What satisfaction in winning, to stroll through the fair dangling a galvanized gallon bucket, evening-bag style, from my arm!

The carneys linger for days after the Fiesta of the Precious Blood is over. They seem content to stay on, even after their customers are few and far between. I suspect they enjoy their time in Teotitlán, a kind of holiday; they can virtually tumble from their makeshift homes into the morning market and emerge with hot-off-the-griddle tlayudas, steaming tamales, whole corn atole, and homemade black mole.

      ꒰꒱꒰꒱꒰꒱

In the cycle of fiestas, the events follow a sequence that weaves an ordered warp and weft to create a familiar pattern repeated over and over again. The first feast in this cycle—the celebration of the Precious Blood of Christ—is also the most complex, and to delve inside its many facets provides understanding for how the feasts of the Virgin of the Nativity and the Virgin of the Rosary similarly unfold.

In September, Teotitlán remounts the magnificent celebrations for the Virgin of the Nativity, who is honored once again in early October, this time manifested as the Virgin of the Rosary. There are cycles within cycles, and every three years the troupe of danzantes finishes its promesa on December 12 with its dance of devotion to Mexico's great mother, the Virgin of Guadalupe.

Festivities get underway with a bedazzling convite. All the participants have assembled, and the roll call is staggering: two full brass bands, nearly two hundred costumed señoritas, the troupe of danzantes in feathers and bells, a pair of masked buffoons, the thirteen members of the Church Committee, and a happy horde of romping youngsters.

Late-afternoon rain clouds threaten as the multitude of stunningly outfitted señoritas converges in the atrium of the church. Each young woman has been invited to participate by one of the thirteen members of the Church Committee,

Hundreds of señoritas carry devotional baskets on their heads for more than a mile. *Gagnier de Mendoza.*

and her position in the procession reflects that particular member's place in the hierarchy. Those invited by the president are more numerous and take their places at the front. It is an honor to be selected for the convite. Participants carry ornately decorated religious standards for more than a half mile, in a combination of public pageantry and religious devotion.

The signal is given, and the spectacle simmers with heightened intensity as the señoritas hoist their *canastas* (baskets) to a perch upon their heads. Both bands share the work during the convite, one toward the front of the procession and the other taking up the rear. While for the most part they take turns playing, they also may simultaneously strike up distinct melodies, creating a fascinating cacophony that must be heard to be appreciated. This sonorous tumult hastens Teotitecos to crowd their doorways, line the street, and surrender to the fleeting excitement, for them something akin to the Rose Bowl Parade.

The troupe of danzantes counterpoises the spectacular assembly of señoritas. In a tantalizing preview of what is to come the following afternoon, the dancers simply walk during the convite. But their measured gait better allows us to appreciate their extravagant attire: massive feathered headdresses encrusted with mirrors, leggings trimmed with swaying fringe and handwoven emblems draped upon their backs. The buffoons romp and prance throughout the orderly convite, stirring up mischief, their antics provoking howls of laughter from the crowds of characteristically reserved Teotitecos.

The Church Committee is responsible for coordinating the convite, and its principal members take up designated positions of importance, while lesser constituents circulate, overseeing the event's progress and distributing posters and tissue-paper flags to the expectant onlookers. Typical of Teotitlán egalitarianism, the convite takes more than an hour to wind through every *sección* of the town. When finally it returns to the church, weary señoritas with aching arms lower their baskets to the ground, to be safely stored within the church until the next convite.

⊡⊡⊡

Fireworks are staged in the church courtyard on the eve of each principal celebration. Vendors sell homemade potato chips, corn on the cob, and meringue-filled sweets. Families arrive in the church's large esplanade with little wooden chairs for the elders and woolen blankets to ward off the cool night air. As the clock nears midnight, the band announces the much-awaited extravaganza.

Pyrotechnic artist Fidencio López from nearby Tlacolula is responsible for the light show featuring seven-foot-tall dolls called *monas*, and others in the form of turkeys and bulls. Daring village men are responsible for dancing them. José Luis Gutiérrez conceals himself within a lightweight reed frame, and with the first notes of the brass band, he transforms the paper and cardboard doll into a breakneck whirling dervish on the verge of takeoff. Fireworks attached to the structure shoot off in all directions and sometimes into the mesmerized crowd. Sparks fly from the turkeys, and sparklers ignite from the bulls' horns—the opening act as anticipation builds toward the grand finale.

The *castillo* is a four-story tower of synchronized fireworks that explode with twirling pinwheels, crackerjack lights, and sizzling silhouettes of the Virgin and Christ on the cross. From the first electrifying spark, the light show continues for some fifteen minutes, concluding with the Virgin's crown disengaging from its pinnacle and ascending to the heavens like a UFO. This is quintessential popular art, made by the people for the people, and like a sign of the times, the popular images of Mickey Mouse and the Virgin Mary coexist on the *castillo,* igniting with equal-opportunity intensity before the crowds.

涄涄涄

It is a Wednesday afternoon in early July, and the Danza de la Pluma is now several hours underway. Today, for the Fiesta of the Precious Blood, the

The papier-mâché *monas* are ready to dance. *Ariel Mendoza.*

The *castillo* explodes with synchronized fireworks. *Ariel Mendoza.*

Gifts of fresh fruit lie at their feet as members of the Church Committee are invited to a *mezcal* during the Danza de la Pluma. *Ariel Mendoza.*

churchyard is clustered with activity, the brass band is nestled under the ancient ficus tree, and the danzantes are performing one impressive leap after another. Seated in the shade are the thirteen members of the Church Committee, the town mayor with his council, and a delegation of the danzantes' fathers. Dozens of folding chairs ring the opposite side of the churchyard, inviting anyone and everyone to watch. The danzantes have sent nets of bananas and cases of apples as an offering, while the municipal authorities have provided cases of half-sized Corona beers and bottles of mezcal. Organization and cooperation sustain these fiestas, serving each other in reciprocal generosity. You won't sit for long before a delegate arrives with bananas or a bottle of beer.

Anguished parents pray to a saint, to the Virgin, or to Christ to heal their sick children, and in return they promise to repay the goodness by signing their sons up to become danzantes. Like most aspects of tradition in Teotitlán, it is not a simple process but an act shrouded in ritual and protocol. In 1996 Celso Ruiz Gutiérrez, age eighteen, was injured in a car accident while driving with his cousin, Leonardo, in California. Both young men had gone north to work. Leonardo did not survive the accident. He died instantly. Celso suffered severe abdominal injuries, including a ruptured spleen, and spent almost four months in the hospital recovering. It was at this time he made a promesa: "I vowed to become a danzante as a way of giving thanks for surviving the accident and becoming strong enough again to dance." The future of the Danza de la Pluma in Teotitlán looks bright, for there is no lack of volunteers. In 2004 the dancer positions were already filled until 2009.

The little girls who accompany Moctezuma in the dance get their positions in a similar fashion. Starting at age seven, Guillermina Ruiz danced for three years in the role of Malintzin, the result of a promesa her parents had made to the Virgin of the Nativity, repaying her for their daughter's miraculous recovery from acute pneumonia.

Becoming a danzante implies an enormous obligation, for both the danzante and his family, during the three full years this compromiso lasts. Like any emperor, the troupe leader who represents the Aztec king Moctezuma has the greatest expenses, as does the Teotil, his next in command. They host grand feasts in their homes and must pay for the band. And when they dance, they dance for the gods. Veteran danzante Manuel Ruiz Martínez passes on his precise knowledge of the complex choreography to the 2004–2006 troupe. They began rehearsing in February 2004, preparing for their debut in July. Like a kaleidoscope, the danzantes move as a group, in and out of ever-changing formations, dropping to their knees only to spiral upward, all the time balancing heavy

The Aztec king is accompanied by two little girls who represent the dual role of the same historical character, Malintzin. *Ariel Mendoza.*

plumed headdresses. This dance is a marathon and is performed as an oblation; in the late 1990s, a troupe danced barefoot during three full years.

The dance was originally acted out in Teotitlán as a theatrical staging of the Spanish victory over Moctezuma and his empire, but by the mid-1990s, there were no takers for the roles of the Spanish conquistador Hernán Cortés and his army. So the Danza de la Pluma was transformed from a true account of history to a singular glorification of native Mexican culture. By no longer sharing the spotlight with the Spaniards, the dancers magnify the splendor of the native kings all the more. But the element of resurgence seems to be a heartening trend in contemporary Teotitlán, and the news going around town is that the Danza de la Pluma troupe confirmed for 2007–2009 will resurrect the Spaniards.

Duality was of utmost importance in pre-Hispanic cosmology, juxtaposing life and death, sun and moon, earth and sky, animal and human—two apparently opposing forces linked to create a whole. The Aztec king Moctezuma represents the sun, and during the dance he is accompanied by two costumed girls who personify this concept of duality. On one side, a girl dressed as an Indian

Dancing for the gods—the *danzantes'* strenuous leaps and turns go on for hours. *Ariel Mendoza.*

portrays Cihuapilli, synonymous with the earth goddess Coatlicue, the sun god's eternal ally. The girl on Moctezuma's other side, clothed as a Spaniard, depicts Malintzin, her attributes corresponding to the moon goddess Coyolxauhqui, in opposition to the sun and Moctezuma's eternal adversary. Both girls portray just one real-life woman who played a pivotal role in Mexican history, both as Moctezuma's subject and as a translator and strategic adviser to the Spanish conquistador Cortés. The dance cleverly suggests her shifting loyalties, as one girl dresses as an Indian princess, and the other wears Western-style clothes.

The small girls dance on several occasions during this daylong endurance event. Whether escorting Moctezuma or dancing on their own, they show surprising stamina with fast-paced cross steps and endless twirls.

罔罔罔

A pair of masked buffoons is indispensable in the Danza de la Pluma. They keep the spectators entertained during breaks between dances: by mimicking onlookers, prancing like the danzantes, and generally clowning around. Their serious work begins when the band starts up and the dancers begin their graceful leaps and turns. These clowns are called *subalternos* (junior officers) and are at the service of the danzantes, performing tasks such as racing home to fetch a more comfortable pair of huaraches. The subalternos are always on the lookout for a danzante in distress, picking up dropped rattles and removing pebbles or debris from the ground. Should any coins hanging from a dancer's necklace fall, the subalternos must find them or personally replace them. If a dancer loses his step, it is the subalternos' job to distract the public from this error.

Ostensibly, no one but the danzantes knows the subalternos' real identities, and indeed they are well concealed behind porcinelike masks encrusted with real pig tusks. These mysterious personages could appear sinister, yet their riotous costumes of yellow and orange and the swishing bobbles fringing their hats offset their evil guises. For the better part of the last twenty years, numerous groups of danzantes have invited Perfecto Mendoza to be one of their subalternos. Perfecto says he prefers older masks. "They are more intriguing to the crowd," he reasons. Therefore, years may go by before a new mask is carved, possibly explaining why such masks are so scarce and seldom part of the most impressive Mexican mask collections.

罔罔罔

The *subalternos* supply comic relief during the hours of dancing but on a serious level are there to assist the *danzantes*. *Ariel Mendoza.*

Dressed in rich brocade and jasmine garlands, this beloved duo, the Virgen de las Posadas and the Virgen del Rosario, are always carried by señoritas. *Ariel Mendoza.*

Just as the bewildering reincarnations of Hindu deities send neophytes into quagmires of confusion, the Catholic manifestations of the Virgin Mary can be equally muddling. The Virgin of Solitude, mourning the death of her son, is dressed in black and holds the Shroud of Turin, yet as the Virgin of Sorrows, she wears an intense shade of purple. In Teotitlán the Virgin of the Nativity wears a light blue gown, and only if you come on February 2, the day of the Candelaria, will you see her carrying the infant Jesus in her arms. Sometimes she stands on a crescent moon. As the Virgin of Guadalupe, she is sustained by a cherub. But each and every image, regardless of costume or accoutrement, represents the same thing—Mary, Mother of God.

Thick auburn locks of human hair fall below the knees of the Virgin of the Nativity, the patroness of Teotitlán. The wig was a gift from a village woman. In the sacristy, a jewelry box is filled with beautiful pearl-studded gold earrings, also gifts of veneration. Only the sacristans have the authority to open the Virgin's niche, touch her, dress her, take her down, and on occasion change her accessories.

In fact, she seldom abandons her niche on the main altarpiece, and it is a rare occasion indeed when she is paraded through the streets of Teotitlán. Antonia Ruiz, now in her mid-sixties, remembers this Virgin leaving the church in a procession only once, and that was a year of extreme drought: "It did not want to rain, and only with the special dispensation of the Church Committee and respected *mayordomos* was she allowed to leave the church. To show our respect, a special canopy shaded her from the sun as the procession moved through the courtyard of the church. After that the rains came quickly." For the Feast of the Virgen de la Natividad, on September 8, the Virgin of the Christmas Posadas heads up the procession, accompanied by the Virgin of the Rosary. Almost exactly one month later, the great mother is honored again, by the Virgen del Rosario dressed in pink.

Before these processions commence, with the statues on palanquins still resting upon on the ground, faithful men and women drape fragrant garlands of *flor de cacao* upon the Virgin's shoulders cloaked in rich brocade. The signal is given, instruments sound, and four señoritas raise each palanquin to their shoulders. Members of the Church Committee hand out bundles of *poleo,* a wild mountain shrub with a refreshing mintlike aroma. Multitudes turn out to accompany their beloved goddesses, and the dusk procession is speckled with candlelit lanterns, homemade confections of blue and white cellophane, colors symbolic of the Virgin Mary. Over and again, the entourage stops at ancient shrines throughout the village core, where the alabanceros drop to their knees to chant before setting forth on a timeless circuit that finally comes full circle well into the night.

A miniature altar for the spirits of *angelitos. Gagnier de Mendoza*

Chapter 8

DEATH AND DAY OF THE DEAD

Life-cycle fiestas are major events in Teotitlán. Baptism and the ensuing celebration officially welcome a new member into the community, while marriage heralds an adult's true coming of age. Death initiates the most radical change of status, from active, flesh-and-blood participant to solely spiritual citizen. To Teotitecos, death is the ultimate rite of passage.

The people of Teotitlán, like most other Zapotecs and native people of Mexico, believe unquestionably in the transcendence of the spirit. Much as we have two eyes and ten fingers, we also have one soul, just as intrinsic a part of our being as the brain and the heart.

While a proper burial gives due importance to the body, this culture places emphasis on the needs of the soul. My husband, Arnulfo, remembers his father's death: "Minutes after my father died, we carried him in and laid him down on the floor right in front of the family altar. We believe that by doing this, the soul of the deceased enters into the earth." Until the last few decades, the homes of most Teotitecos had clay floors, and although shiny tile now paves most altar rooms in the village, "floor" still translates to "earth," thus even tile floors retain the ability to cradle the soul. "It is on this spot that we place a crucifix, and it becomes a kind of home base for the soul until the ninth day," explains Arnulfo.

El velorio is the wake. The name comes from the word *velar,* meaning "to stand guard," and in Teotitlán the *difunto* ("deceased"; in Spanish the word connotes a certain personalized affection) is in the constant company of the living during this time. In this tropical climate where embalming is little used, the wake is expedited with considerable efficiency. It usually lasts no more than thirty-six hours. According to local custom, mourners must keep one entire night of vigil before burying the difunto. Therefore, someone dying at 2:00 a.m. would be buried in the afternoon a day and a half later. But if the death occurs at 2:00 p.m., the funeral would be the next day, since the *velorio* would take in an entire night.

Although the *velorio* is a time to talk and reminisce about the difunto, it is also a time to talk *to* the difunto! There is a common belief that the difunto can hear all that is said during the wake and throughout the funeral procession, right up to the threshold of the cemetery gates. It is at this pivotal point that loved ones say their last good-byes, for it is believed that once the coffin crosses into the cemetery, the difunto loses all memory of his or her earlier life (only temporarily, that is, as will become clear in exploring the Day of the Dead).

I like to see this grand sendoff as a giant farewell party, much like that given for a loved one moving far away. This is a major get-together, where the best food is prepared and a brass band plays. A funeral in Teotitlán is an astounding act of community cooperation, and commissions are set up to see to every detail.

Adolescents and single men chop firewood and acquire extra water. Teams of young women turn tortilla making into an efficient production-line process, one pressing the masa while the other oversees its cooking on the hot *comal*. Older women, in keeping with the established hierarchy, prepare meals and make hot chocolate. Every married couple attending a *velorio* makes an offering to the difunto by placing white flowers and a simple large candle or a *veladora* (paraffin votive candle) on or near the altar. To help out with the expenses, mourners bring mezcal and several pounds of dried corn kernels when arriving in the day, or a basket of bread if they come after dark. Close family members make the greatest contributions, including sacks of sugar and maize, costly cacao beans, or cash.

Just before the funeral procession leaves the home en route to the cemetery, the difunto is equipped with essential travel aids for his or her upcoming journey. Loved ones tuck into the coffin indispensable items: holy water stored in a hollow length of bamboo for protection from mishaps along the way, and thirteen pairs of tiny tortillas to feed the mysterious black dog that guides souls to the afterlife, both traditions linked to ancient native beliefs. No example better illustrates the syncretism between pre-Hispanic beliefs and Catholicism, Teotitlán's pervading religion, than the ritual transformation of cacao, a native plant of Mexico. In pre-Hispanic Mexico, cacao was served unsweetened as a bitter elixir, reserved for the upper echelons of society. It was also a form of money, and the dead were buried with precious cacao beans to pay tolls along the mythological river they traveled to get to the "other side." Today the "other side" implies heaven—hopefully—and Teotitlán's difuntos are buried with rounds of sweetened chocolate and an old coin cut in quarters to pay for travel costs.

Although the burial marks the difunto's physical absence from the home and family, in keeping with Oaxacan beliefs, the soul has not yet fully departed. *Los nueve días* (the nine days), initiated at the burial and ending with the *levantada de la cruz* (taking up of the cross) nine days later, are a particularly delicate time for the fragile soul making its difficult and dangerous journey to the other world. During these nine days, the soul is in a liminal state, at the threshold of the afterlife, waiting on God's decision: the good fortune of going directly to heaven, the common option of paying for minor sins with a stint in purgatory, or the remote possibility of condemnation in hell.

Prayer plays a key role in the rituals surrounding *los nueve días*. According to Catholic belief, the difunto's time in purgatory can be reduced or eliminated through the intercession of prayer on the part of the living (likewise, through their proximity to the gods, the dead are believed capable of influencing the lives of those in the earthly realm). At this precarious time of transition for the soul, the living can help the newly deceased with nightly prayers, aiding their transformation from matter to energy and their trip from the here and now to the

Granddaughters pay their last respects to the spirit of Victoria González. *Gagnier de Mendoza.*

other side. Several alabanceros sing together, and it is a profound experience to hear the deep harmony of the *alabanzas,* those ancient prayers that resonate in the souls of both the living and the dead. Close relatives and compadres attend the *alabanzas,* their presence showing support to both the difunto and the grieving family. Mezcal, hot chocolate, and bread are served late into the night to fortify participants and observers during this nightly ritual.

On the ninth day, close family members bear witness to the visually dramatic ritual of the *levantada de la cruz.* A few days prior to the "taking up," village specialists create a *tapete* (rug) of sand about three by six feet and decorated with colored sawdust. The tapete is constructed on the same spot where the difunto was laid shortly after death; after reposing in the earth, the soul now rises into the tapete. At this gathering of family members, echoes of the funeral return with the alabanceros' mournful tones and the band's solemn dirges. The ritual begins as family members file up to sprinkle holy water on the tapete and kiss the crucifix at its base. The event palpates with drama, and five people are chosen to sweep up the tapete. As it is taboo for the difunto's immediate family or godchildren to perform the task, most often godparents and relatives are chosen. The tapete is divided into five numbered sections, corresponding to the four limbs of the cross with the fifth section at its center. The alabanceros chant prayers, indicating the order in which the cross is to be taken up. It is considered bad luck to scoop up the contents with bare hands, so people use dried corn husks instead. Section by section, the entire tapete is deposited into a bucket, until the last remaining grain of sand is swept from the floor. This act symbolizes not only the soul's final departure but also the removal of all remnants of death from the home, signaling a return to normal life.

Nine days after death, the remains of the sand rug, now the physical repository of the soul, repeat the funeral procession through the streets of Teotitlán, pausing at the church for blessings before arriving at the cemetery. The remains, a bucket of sand and sawdust, are poured into a channel carved in the form of a cross upon the simple earthen grave, symbolically reuniting body and soul.

回回回

It is essential to understand the indigenous Catholic viewpoint to appreciate the potent traditions surrounding the death of a child. According to Catholic doctrine, baptism erases the original sin inherited by children from their parents. Having not yet reached the age of conscious action, children die free of sin, speeding straight to heaven to enjoy an eternal afterlife in paradise,

On the ninth day after a death, family and friends sweep up the cross. The author's mother-in-law, Clara, waits her turn, as Tía Reyna sweeps up her part of the sand rug, made for their friend and neighbor Victoria González. *Gagnier de Mendoza.*

For the Day of the Dead, an earthen grave is marked with simple offerings. *Ariel Mendoza.*

thus becoming angelitos. In keeping with this belief, parents of dead children should not grieve, for no longer do their children suffer. "We weren't supposed to mourn because the Virgin had chosen our angelito," explains my Tía Antonia, remembering her last child's funeral. "After we returned from the cemetery, according to custom, the band played fiesta music, and even as the tears rolled down my cheeks, I had to dance."

Until 1960, everyone in Teotitlán danced at a child's funeral. It was Pedro, who lived by the creek, who changed this tradition. He said, "How is it possible for me to dance and be happy when my child has just died?" Although no one dances anymore at an angelito's funeral, the tradition of playing lively, upbeat music persists. Parents feel a deep sense of responsibility to properly marry off their children, and everyone I spoke with agreed that the festive atmosphere substitutes for the wedding the parents would have one day given had the child lived to be married. The angelito's godparents are responsible for buying the child's farewell outfit. He or she is dressed in white, a symbol of purity and the customary color for baptisms, first communions, and wedding gowns.

In an excerpt from the 1951 novel *La Mayordomía,* written by Oaxacan Rogelio Barrigan and set in Tlacolula, a neighboring Zapotec town, we can see how a culture's strong established customs clash with its people's own irrepressible emotions:

> In the patio the music had begun to play a festive march, while Pedro, the husband, along with his compadre Celestino, attends to the guests, circulating with excessive frequency the bottle of mezcal and the jug of tepache. Juana is indignant when the music starts up, as if it were a fandango wedding or a mayordomía fiesta, but she bites her tongue knowing that no one will listen to her complaints, since it is the custom of the village to throw a fiesta when a little one dies. Tía Chana, both for her years and wisdom of people, is aware of Juana's opposing view and tries to console her, "We should be happy, Juana. What greater luck than to die at this age, never knowing the bitterness of this world! Your son has gone straight to heaven!"
>
> Juana knows very well that the soul of her little Lenchito will be in heaven, yet in spite of this, she cannot enjoy the fiesta.

The people of Teotitlán are widely recognized as exemplary hosts, anxious to attend to their guests in grand style. On Día de Muertos (Day of the Dead) on November 2, visiting spirits receive a truly royal reception. Preparations have been in the making for days. Normally industrious Teotitlán comes to a grinding halt for this fiesta, and as Tía Antonia warns, "No one should work while the spirits are still visiting!"

Angels and saints have much in common, and they certainly reside in the same heavenly abode. So appropriately, the angelitos return on November 1, All Saints' Day. As with most indigenous feast days, the celebration actually begins the day before. Beginning at noon on October 31, the villagers attend to the souls of children, who depart just after the first adult spirits begin arriving at 3:00 p.m. on November 1. Officially, the adult souls take leave at 3:00 p.m. on November 2, but should this day fall on a Sunday, the day liturgically reserved for the Lord, the souls must wait until November 3.

〰〰〰

It is midday, November 1, and many years have passed since Antonia Ruiz lost her last child. This spirited, compact woman shares her views about Día de Muertos and the traditions surrounding the return of the small spirits. She speaks from firsthand experience; she has buried five of her eleven children. She leads me past the newly renovated altar room, through the porch, and into her daughters' bedroom. I am initially perplexed to be moving away from the main altar room, but as we enter into the cool darkness, a small altar does emerge.

Incense, candles, and flowers: ever-present symbols on the Day of the Dead altar. *Ariel Mendoza.*

Antonia explains that this was the original *sala* (parlor) and part of the home built by her husband's parents forty years before. It had been the home's ceremonial center until 1980, when Antonia and her husband, Félix, built their own *sala*. She says she still maintains this small altar because it was here, in this room, that they held wakes when her own small children died. "This is the place they know. This is where they come back to. We attend the spirits here," explains Antonia, while her daughter Reyna lowers from the altar offerings left for the children's spirits. Peanuts and pecans, tiny egg breads, miniature china cups filled with hot chocolate, and the tiny bars of chocolate used for making this essential beverage all form the traditional *ofrenda* (offering) in Teotitlán. "While the angelitos are here we often hear the sound of clacking ceramics coming from this room," interjects Reyna, "the same sound made when taking a drink and placing the cup back in the saucer."

By mid-afternoon the spirits of adults have arrived. My mother-in-law, Clara, is busy attending to four visitors in her *sala* when another couple arrives. On a day like today, with so much coming and going, she has left her main entrance open. Her sister-in-law Leonora and her husband, Renaldo, enter the room quietly, while the other guests fall into a respectful silence. The couple goes directly to the altar, unpacking from a large basket their ofrenda of bread, fruit, nuts, and a single taper almost three feet tall. Leonora's candle, now lighted, joins rank with six others on the floor, at the base of the altar, illuminating a framed photograph of Emiliano, Clara's deceased husband. According to custom, the

Aromatic wildflowers frame this *ofrenda* to Julián Mendoza. *Gagnier de Mendoza.*

couple kneels respectfully before the altar, and only now that the difuntos have been properly greeted do the guests direct their attentions to the living—first to Clara and then to her adult sons and the other guests. They take their place at the large table, and comfortable conversation resumes.

The spirits want constant company during their brief twenty-four-hour visit. While virtually every home has its own spirits to attend to, in a tight-knit community like Teotitlán, most folks spend a good part of the fiesta paying their respects to spirit relatives at others' homes.

Hours later Clara instructs her grown children to keep watch over the altar and attend to any visitors while she goes off to visit the homes of several relatives. In a sturdy reed basket tucked under her rebozo, she carries a bottle of mezcal, half a dozen egg breads, and several blocks of chocolate. She will return home more than once to replenish the offerings in the course of her obligatory rounds. Her first stop is the home of her deceased mother-in-law; the door is open. She glides silently through the courtyard, entering directly into the *sala*. Ignoring the other guests seated at the long table, she moves directly to the altar. She kisses the edge of the altar, then kneels to pray. I asked my mother-in-law what she prayed for at this moment. "May the spirit of the deceased be at peace," she replied. When she rises, she greets her brother-in-law Andrés Ruiz, who, as the youngest son and concurrent with Zapotec custom, still occupies his moth-

Clara's altar barely balances the offerings of *mole negro,* chocolate, fruit, and bread. *Gagnier de Mendoza.*

er's home. Emerging from the kitchen, Andrés's wife, Meche, takes a position beside her husband and receives the loaded basket from Clara. This same scene has been played out countless times before, and Meche moves automatically to the altar to distribute the offerings. This is just one example of the deep sense of compromiso—the obligation to perform one's duty—within this community.

Antonia and Félix explained their vision of the spirits' comings and goings during Día de Muertos: "Sometimes the spirits come to visit with friends or maybe with a compadre. They also visit other homes apart from where they lived and died. They go to the homes of their children, godparents, and favorite relatives." So while the living make their rounds, paying their respects to the spirits of loved ones, bringing baskets laden with *pan de muertos* (Day of the Dead bread), peanuts and apples, tamales and mezcal, likewise the spirits have an open invitation to enjoy the aromas rising from other altars.

Even young couples living in new homes, where no one they know has died, prepare ofrendas, partly for an unknown spirit who might return to its ancestral site and partly for the soul of a family member or godparent who might come to visit. Should they need to leave their house empty during Muertos, this awkward situation can be partially remedied by leaving the door to the altar room open. This act is symbolic of inviting the souls in to visit.

Even worse than poorly attending to the spirits is not receiving them at all, and Teotitecos have much to say on this matter. Antonia remembers that when she was a young girl, her family moved to a large piece of land in the heart of the village: "Many people had lived and died on this land long before we came to it, but for years it had been abandoned. When our first Día de Muertos arrived, in the early hours of November 2, my mother heard moans out in the big yard." Victoria González, at 4:00 a.m., went out in the dark to reassure the sad souls. "Don't cry anymore. We are going to take care of all of you," she consoled them, assuring them they were welcome. "Even if we don't have much to give you, please join us." Each November for almost half a century, the unknown souls have been contented, and never a mysterious moan has been heard since.

囘囘囘

Only the best is offered to the dead, and at 3:00 p.m. on November 1, as the church bells signal the spirits' arrival, the living put the finishing touches on their altars. These days there is a lot to go around. Antonia's three daughters are busy in the kitchen. Reyna pours a cup of hot chocolate whipped to a thick froth and nestles it among three large *pan de muertos*. Elia deftly mounds steaming tamales on a platter, while Alta Gracia ladles black mole over a poached turkey leg. Antonia runs a tight ship and has strategically placed the chocolate, tamales, and mole on her altar, anticipating by minutes the arrival of *los muertos*.

"But things were not always like this," emphasizes Félix Mendoza, comfortably presiding over the goings-on. According to custom, he sits closest to the altar, at a long wooden table he made himself, his back to the wall and gazing at the doorway. This trim, handsome man in his late fifties, dashing with a well-groomed mustache and thick head of hair, has seen more changes in half a century than any Zapotec ancestor since the arrival of the Spaniards. Félix remembers, "I would work day and night to finish weaving a sarape before Muertos. I'd take it to sell in the Tlacolula market, and there were times when after an entire day in the sun, I returned home with the unsold piece. Now, we were really desperate! If I didn't sell the sarape, we would have nothing to offer our difuntos—not mole, not turkey, not even chocolate! My only option left was to sell it to one of the wholesalers in the village, who in those days would pay us whatever they wanted, sometimes only half the value of the weaving because they knew we were in a bind." Like the rest of the folks in Teotitlán and most indigenous people in Mexico, Félix and Antonia learned their customs and rituals from their own parents, and their sense of obligation to carry on these traditions is unwavering when it comes to attending to the dead.

My husband, Arnulfo, tells a story that his father told him. In the early 1950s, just before Arnulfo's parents' first Day of the Dead as a married couple, his father could not sell the rug he had finished weaving to cover the expenses of the fiesta. He had to find a way to make an offering to the dead, so he took his burro up into the mountains to cut the tiny white aromatic flowers that are found only in the northern sierra of Teotitlán. With their burro laden, the young couple set off to neighboring villages, trading the sweet flowers for bread, corn, and beans, acceptable offerings in those lean times.

Just as flashing lights on a runway guide an airplane in, so the elements on a family altar reassure a spirit that it has come to the right home. Photographs, as correct as possible, are central to the arrangement. A simple glass of water is perhaps the most indispensable offering on any Day of the Dead altar. As with the souls' first arduous journeys to the other world, the trip back home is also arduous, and they need water to quench their thirst. Candles also play an important symbolic role, and Alejandrina Ríos, Tía Antonia's daughter-in-law, believes that "candles illuminate the spirits' path on their return. If you offer no candles, then they light their *deditos* (little fingers) to better see the rocks and thorns that line the dark road back." Could this be why candles are also lit on the grave both immediately following burial and again at the Day of the Dead, a time of travel in the spirit world?

Clara's Day of the Dead altar—a magnificent homage to the spirits of the dead. *Ariel Mendoza.*

Mole de Castilla

This recipe comes from Tía Natalia's original recipe for mole for five hundred. Here it's been reduced to serve twelve. This is not a fiery-hot dish. It should be very flavorful but mild enough to eat like a thick stew.

2 medium-sized chickens or 1 small turkey, cut into serving pieces

2 large white onions, peeled and quartered

1 pound *guajillo* chiles (substitute ancho chiles), split in half down the sides and seeded

1 cup lightly packed fresh oregano (leaves only)

1/4 cup lightly packed fresh thyme (leaves only)

3 1/2 tablespoons whole cloves, coarsely ground with mortar and pestle or spice grinder

35 whole allspice berries, coarsely ground with mortar and pestle or spice grinder

10 heads native Mexican garlic (small cloves) or 6 heads large garlic, skins left on

3/4 cup whole cumin, finely ground with mortar and pestle or spice grinder

sea salt to taste

25 dense bread rolls, slowly oven-toasted at 200°F until very dr.

3 avocados, used for garnish

In large stock pot, add 10 quarts water, onions, 2 teaspoons salt, and chicken or turkey pieces. Bring to a simmer.

Simmer for 30 minutes or until poultry is tender. Skim any foam that rises to the surface.

Remove meat and cool. Strain stock and reserve.

On a *comal* or griddle, toast garlic cloves over medium heat until skins are blackened in spots and garlic is soft. Allow to cool. Peel skins.

On the same *comal,* toast chiles, taking care not to burn them.

Soak toasted chiles in hot water until softened, approximately 10 minutes.

Toast chile seeds, moving constantly until golden. Allow to cool briefly.

With a mortar and pestle or spice grinder, grind seeds to a fine consistency. Reserve in a small bowl.

In a blender, combine half the chiles, drained of their soaking water, with 1 cup reserved broth or water. Process from low to high speed for 1 minute, until very smooth. Repeat this process with the other chiles.

Strain through a fine metal sieve in batches, gently knocking edge of sieve. Push out excess paste with the back of a large spoon. Discard pulp.

In a blender, combine oregano, thyme, cloves, allspice, cumin, garlic, and 1 cup water or broth. Process from low to high speed for 1 minute, to the consistency of thin cake batter.

In 6 quarts simmering chicken stock, stir constantly while pouring in the spice paste, three-quarters of the chile paste, and half the ground chile seeds. Bring to a boil, taste, and adjust salt. Add more paste and ground seeds for a hotter flavor. If you add more paste or seeds, allow the mole to come to a second boil.

Simmer for 30 minutes, stirring occasionally, and adjust salt.

Break dried bread rolls into 1-inch-square chunks.

Reheat chicken pieces in 1 quart stock.

Slowly add bread chunks to mole, stirring very gently but constantly. Stir slowly over low heat for 15 more minutes. Add more stock as needed. The consistency should be thick but not stiff.

Ladle sauce over heated chicken in a bowl or deep plate. Serve with hot tortillas and fresh avocado slices

Antonia and Félix offer steaming bowls of *mole de castilla* to their visiting spirits. *Gagnier de Mendoza.*

Just a stone's throw away, the grand altar at Clara's home takes first prize for its sheer abundance. On the edge of the altar rise two-foot-high layers of *pan de muertos*, reminiscent of mortarless fieldstone walls. Here is a true balancing act, the breads topped with plates of apples, oranges, and tamales. So high is this arrangement that the Mendoza family's saintly entourage, protected within wooden niches, is barely visible peaking over the oven-browned mounds.

For a woman in her mid-sixties, Clara moves industriously from altar room to patio to kitchen, intent on properly attending to her guests. The woman, like a miraculous apparition, appears serving bowls of scalding atole, hot chocolate, and steaming tamales. After 1:00 p.m., she dispenses with the atole and chocolate, drinks associated with breakfast, switching to *mole de Castilla,* her deceased husband Emiliano's favorite dish. As the shadows grow longer, new guests arrive while others leave, unnecessarily explaining that they must cut their visits short, having many homes to visit during this busy day.

Aroma is to the spirits what taste is to the living, and the intense smells satiate the *muertos,* while the living indulge in bowls of rich turkey mole and steaming *tamales de mole amarillo.* The heady incense of copal and the tiny scented wildflowers that bloom for Muertos are essential elements on any Teotitlán altar. It is believed that the spirits can absorb the essence of the food, thus the living prepare very aromatic dishes. Villagers often comment that bread taken off an altar weighs less than it did when first placed there, or that food removed from an ofrenda has no flavor left. Respected village elder Marino Vásquez explains: "When the difuntos feast on the spirit of the food, they take away its essence." The family seldom eats food from the altar, yet nothing goes to waste. The pigs dine well.

"It isn't just food we offer to the difuntos. We buy them presents, too!" Antonia confirms. Tiny sugar sheep, turkeys, and angels, decorated with colored frosting, are made especially for the altars of angelitos. Some families add miniature objects to the altars—metates and tortilla presses for daughters, and toy hammers and hoes for sons. "Every year we buy a brand-new *tenate* (woven basket), *molcajete* (mortar and pestle), and *jarrito* (clay jug). Sure, we use them afterward, but the spirits do take the gifts away symbolically. We know that," Antonia explains, "because women who have gone to wash clothes in the river before the fiesta is over testify, in spite of their fright, to seeing difuntos leading away pack burros or carrying baskets under their arms and sacks over their shoulders loaded with ofrendas."

Marino explains that if the spirits like to drink *mezcalito,* then a toast is made. The *juez* (official mezcal server) will first pour a shot of mezcal and drizzle it in the form of the cross on the ofrenda at the foot of the altar. Only after a

For the Day of the Dead, Antonia and her daughter Reyna prepare *tamales de mole amarillo* for the spirits and the living. *Gagnier de Mendoza.*

On November 2, this couple sees off their spirits, sharing some fruit and quiet time. *Ariel Mendoza.*

mezcalito has been offered to the difunto will the *juez* pass out shooters to all the visitors at the table, in order of hierarchy.

Many villagers insist on "seeing off" their loved ones at the cemetery, much like taking someone to the airport rather than calling a taxi. Others, like Félix and Antonia, never go to the cemetery on November 2. Félix is quick to justify his actions, saying that going to the cemetery would be like kicking the spirits out of the house. Some spirits leave slowly and others get drunk, so the fiesta spills over to November 3.

At three in the afternoon on November 2, deafening firecrackers explode from the churchyard and homes, signaling to the entire populace, both living and dead, that it is time for the souls to think about their journey back. A visit to the cemetery on this same afternoon is a sight to behold; the graves dance with enormous bunches of deep red cockscomb and brilliant marigolds, the arrangements accented with delicate white calla lilies. Many families go to the cemetery bearing fruits, peanuts, bottles of mezcal, and cases of beer. This is a time to clean the tombstones; some families even diligently scrub them with soap and water. They light candles and make long-winded toasts to departing loved ones. If the graveyard is to the spirit what the airport departure lounge is to the earthly traveler, the spirits that come to Teotitlán for Day of the Dead get a first-class send-off all the way. In early November, the warm glowing rays of the late-afternoon sun heighten the intense tones of the flowers, and as one nears the cemetery's tiny chapel, the woeful chants of the alabanceros invite those present to indulge in the moment's sweet sorrow.

The band plays emotive dirges and slow marches, the same sad songs played for a funeral procession, which every villager has accompanied on countless occasions, escorting close and extended family on their last and ultimate rite of passage, the journey we will all one day make to the "other side."

Just as Sunday is dedicated to the Lord, every Monday in November belongs to the dead. For five weeks, Padre Rómulo, who attends to the spiritual needs of Teotitlán as well as four other nearby villages, visits each community in turn, celebrating *los responsos* in each cemetery. On the Monday designated for Teotitlán, even those who remained home with the languishing souls on November 2 will likely visit the cemetery, giving the priest a small donation, for which he will recite individual prayers at the graves of departed loved ones. The exuberance of fresh flowers and the soulful harmonies heighten the senses, enabling them to take in every detail of this moment, suspended in time and space, somewhere between heaven and earth.

Every three years, the *danzantes* end their term by dancing for the Virgen de Guadalupe. Family members accompany the fiesta with lavishly decorated *jicapextles*. *Ariel Mendoza.*

EPILOGUE

As I write these words I hear music floating up the hill from the village. Day after day it announces each passing event of the year and preserves a diary of Teotitlán. The *chirimía*'s ancient tones evoke the mood of rituals. During processions, the instrument's piercing wails precede the wood and stucco deities, so lovingly protected beneath the palanquin's canopy. Music is synonymous with fiestas, solemn or exuberant, whether centered in the church or the family home. Five full brass bands, more than 150 musicians (men and in recent years women), mark the rhythms of the year in Teotitlán.

This New Year's Day, a band played *jarabes* in the home of the godparents of the baby Jesus. Before the next day's dawn, Nabor Gutiérrez, a huehuete who only hours before presided over the dances, died in his sleep. Funerary dirges— stirring songs of ancient origin—filled the night air, alternating with the ala-banceros' moving chants. The following day, as the sun hung low in the winter sky, a man whose life as a huehuete had been a cornerstone to village ritual, over-seeing countless weddings, ceremonies to content, and courtly *mayordomías,* was accompanied, with music, candles, flowers, and mezcal, on one last promenade through the streets, a stirring prelude to his burial. Today the sun set with sounds of mourning, and in a timeless cycle of renewal, it rose with the next dawn to the upbeat marches of a wedding procession.

On December 11, on the eve of the Feast of the Virgin of Guadalupe, masses of yellow wildflowers, freshly cut on forays into the surrounding moun-tains, seemingly float toward the morning market. With enormous bundles bal-anced upon their heads, Teotitlán women, examples of perfect posture, glide through the streets, while young men push flower-filled wheelbarrows, and sturdy donkeys plod along, virtually concealed beneath their floral loads. They are all headed for the market. All the while, women emerge from the market, each embracing her purchase, bouquets of the same yellow flowers that will dress with dignity the family altars of Teotitlán, a fitting decoration to celebrate their much-revered Virgin.

The historic apparition of the Virgen de Guadalupe, Mary, Mother of God, occurred within twenty-five years of the Spanish conquest of Mexico. She appeared on a mound in present-day Mexico City, where just years before had stood a temple to the beloved pre-Hispanic goddess Tonantzin. For a polytheistic culture that adopted and discarded gods with each new invader, it could be said that their venerable Tonantzin had just changed outfits. Her new name became Guadalupe, and to this day she provides, to these agrarian people, an essential link with the benevolent Mother Earth.

On December 12, 2003, the danzantes perform for the Virgen de Guadalupe. After dark their extended families gather in the esplanade of the church. The danzantes are finishing their three-year promesa, and their last dance is for the primal goddess. She is the catalyst for the commencement of a new cycle, a link with the dead—who only a month before returned to the spirit world—and the impending birth of both the infant God and the new year. Then it is the women's turn to dance with their richly decorated jicapextles. These giant gourds, carefully arranged with handmade sugar flowers, are reserved for only the most important festive dances.

Just as yellow wildflowers honor the Virgen de Guadalupe, one month later, Teotitlán dresses its altars with fragrant rosemary and native red poinsettias to honor the miraculous Black Christ of Esquipulas. The verses of this unending song resound on February 2, the day of the Candelaria, when Teotitecos bring their seeds to be blessed at the church; gourds and baskets hold seeds carefully saved from previous harvests and destined for the upcoming planting. Not only seeds are blessed on this day. The infant Jesus sits up after reclining in the family Nativity since December 24 and is brought to the church. My sisters-in-law Rosario and Rufina join a steady stream of the faithful, each embracing their own infant gods, lovingly dressed in velvet and brocade. They are waiting for the priest's benediction.

The year continues with music, the steadfast marker of every feast. Like the bitter richness of a toasted cacao bean, the suffering through the intense heat of the Good Friday procession is great. In an outpouring of empathy, this devotional suffering mirrors the suffering that Christ endured as he carried the cross, and the suffering of his mourning mother. Ice cream stalls bring relief from

Even the children in Teotitlán dance for the gods. *Ariel Mendoza.*

the heat and promise to cool intense emotions. Countless families, all witnesses to the passion play, depart the churchyard and, relieved of their penitent solemnity, joyously partake of cactus fruit ices and exotic burned-milk sherbets.

Like an encore, the Danza de los Viejos follows the intensity of Holy Week. With both levity and impressive communal organization, each neighborhood hosts for a day the masked viejos, who dance through the streets and into the plaza, bringing entertainment to the entire community.

The rains come in summer, when Teotitlán honors it patron saints, the Precious Blood of Christ and the Virgin Mother. For this, a brass band embarks on another musical marathon of unmistakable polkas and waltzes, counterpoised by the masterful leaps and twirls of Teotitlán's troupe of danzantes.

Life in Teotitlán—an echo of native Mexico—is a mystical dance of cycles ending and others beginning, overlapping with intriguing complexities and layered in the juicy, rich syncretism of the folk traditions of ancient Spain and thriving Zapotec culture.

The *viejos* arrive at our yearly Fiesta de la Santa Cruz on May 3. *Ariel Mendoza.*

EPILOGUE

Teotitecos, although dependent on the commerce of rug weaving, take the time, often days, to participate in fiestas, where they rally together with gusto and goodwill to celebrate their own people and their gods and to confirm their sense of place and purpose. By working, eating, drinking, and dancing together, they sustain a sense of identity that could easily crumble under economic competition and business jealousies.

In a tightly knit community like Teotitlán, where with rare exception everyone either has been raised within its ranks or has married in, an intricate protocol has evolved, leaving little to haphazard occurrence. People still greet each other in the streets, and at morning market, multitudes of women stop to enfold one another's hands, uttering the primordial *chxan* with each gesture. This respectful greeting interweaves the sacred through mundane encounters and fiesta ceremonies.

One day, as I sit listening to Marino Vásquez speak about his village, we hear the deep, resonant ring of the largest church bell, followed in close succession by two short rings of a higher pitch. "A woman has died," he tells me. Like all adults in Teotitlán, Marino understands the "dialect" of the church bells, a kind of Morse code that announces, among a multitude of messages, deaths, weddings, calls to Mass, the end of fasting, and the birth of the new year. As if to clarify the matter, he adds, "Had a man died, the bell would have rung twice low and once high." That night, the air was drenched in the melancholy sounds of mourning—and quite possibly awakened the very next day to the festive tones of a wedding procession.

Glossary

abuela: a grandmother or any elderly woman.

alabanceros: ritual chanters who sing prayers (*alalanzas*).

ancho chiles: large mild poblano chiles, dried once.

atole: a hot and hearty breakfast beverage, usually made from corn.

baúl: a hope chest.

bejuco: a vine.

Candelaria: in Oaxaca, the day people take their seeds and their statue of the baby Jesus, sitting up in a chair, to be blessed at the church.

cargo: a designated civil or religious office with the local government; usually a nonpaying position.

chintextle: a chile and garlic paste.

chocolate atole: a fiesta beverage featuring cacao beans transformed through anaerobic fermentation, and white corn *atole*.

chxan: the Zapotec word approximating *God;* said as a greeting of respect.

comadre: a term of address used by a child's parents to his or her godmother.

comida: the main meal of the day, eaten between 2:00 and 3:00 p.m.

comidera: a woman in charge of supervising meals prepared for fiestas.

compadrazgos: relationships with the godparents of one's children or with the parents of one's godchildren.

comadre, compadre: a term of address used between the godparents and parents of the godchild.

compromiso: a commitment; an obligatory engagement.

consuegros: the parents of one's son-in-law or daughter-in-law.

convite: the procession that announces a religious fiesta.

copal: tree resin burned as incense.

copitas: shooters, typically used for drinking *mezcal*.

danzón: a popular dance of Cuban origin.

enredo: a native wrap skirt.

faja: a sash cinched at the waist.

fandango: the most elaborate of weddings by Teotitlán standards.

guajillo chile: a mild dried chile.

guelaguetza: a reciprocal system of loaning goods.

huehuete: a ritual master of ceremonies.

ikat: fabric in which the yarns have been tie-dyed before weaving.

invitados: invited guests; extended family who not only attend a fiesta but also help out with the work.

jarabe: Mexico's national dance.

jicapextle: a lacquered gourd.

jota: a Spanish folk dance from the region of Aragón.

marimba: a kind of wooden xylophone.

mayordomía: a religious celebration for a local saint, the Virgin, or Christ, sponsored by individuals.

mayordomos: sponsors of religious celebrations.

mecapal: tumpline; a strap fastened to a load and around the forehead, to lift the load for carrying on the back.

metate: a three-footed rectangular grinding stone, used with a stone cylinder.

mezcal: a distilled alcohol made from maguey (agave).

Mitla: a pre-Hispanic archaeological site near Teotitlán, renowned for its richly carved facade.

mole: a spicy sauce.

pan dulce: sweet bread that comes in a variety of forms.

pasodoble: a two-step dance.

petate: a woven palm floor mat.

piquete: a shot of liquor; literally a "sting."

posadas: pre-Christmas folk celebrations held from December 16 to December 24.

rebozo: a woman's traditional shawl.

responsos: prayers for the dead.

San Isidro: the patron saint of farmers.

santo: a saint; a statue of a saint.

secciones: neighborhoods. There are five *secciones* in Teotitlán.

Teotitecos: the people of Teotitlán.

tepache: a mildly fermented drink.

tía/tío: aunt/uncle.

tlayuda: a large corn tortilla.

tortilla: a corn flat bread; a staple of the native Mexican diet.

viejos: elders; the masked personages who appear following Easter Sunday.